MATH SERIES

Fractions

MASTERY

A Breath of Fresh Air

Garlic Press

Please contact Garlic Press directly for reproduction rights that include
classroom use, parental instruction, or community organizations.

Published by
Garlic Press
605 Powers St.
Eugene, OR 97402

ISBN: 978-1-930820-68-5
Order Number GP-168
Printed in China

www.garlicpress.com

TABLE OF CONTENTS

An Approach to Fractions...4

Chapter 1: **Whole Numbers** 5
    Factors 5
    Composite & Prime Numbers 7
    Greatest Common Factor 11
    Common Multiples 14
    Chapter Review 18

Chapter 2: **Introducing Fractions** 19
    Equivalent Fractions 21
    Reducing Fractions.. 23
    Common Denominators 25
    Chapter Review 28

Chapter 3: **Addition** 29
    Addition with Common Denominators.................................... 29
    Addition with Unlike Denominators 34
    Chapter Review 39

Chapter 4: **Subtraction** 40
    Subtraction with Common Denominators 40
    Subtraction with Unlike Denominators.................................. 43
    Chapter Review 48

Chapter 5: **Multiplication**.. 49
    Multiplying Fractions by Fractions 49
    Multiplying Fractions, Whole Numbers & Mixed Numbers......... 49
    Cross Cancellation.. 51
    Chapter Review 55

Chapter 6: **Division**... 56
    Reciprocals 56
    Chapter Review 59

Final Assessment Test... 60

Answers 61

An Approach to Fractions

Understanding fractions proceeds best in a balance of three stages: using manipulatives for concrete representations; using pictorials as semi-concrete representations; and, finally, using numbers to represent abstract relationships involving procedures and operations.

Manipulatives provide a learner with a concrete way to make a physical model of an abstract mathematical idea. A learner is then able to connect his or her discoveries to a mathematical vocabulary and to mathematical symbols. Pictorial representations use graphs, diagrams, and the like as a next step in development. Pictorials are semi-concrete, not the physical objects of manipulation, but pictures or visual representations of ideas.

Fractions Mastery focuses on the last stage involving numbers, procedures, and operations. This is not a book of manipulatives or pictorial representations. This book follows from them, into higher levels of abstract concepts and algorithms. The book will present step-by-step procedures involving a variety of operations (addition, subtraction, multiplication, division) as each applies to fractions.

Each section of this book addresses a concept important to fractions mastery. Explanations are made, clear examples are given, and exercises provide for practice and mastery. Periodic testing can be used as a simple assessment tool to measure how well a learner has understood a presented concept. All of this is done within the standards for Numbers and Operations described by the National Council of Teachers of Mathematics, with special attention to understanding numbers, understanding the meanings of operations, and computing fluently.

This book is arranged in six chapters. Chapters 1 and 2 provide prerequisite background skills that involve fractions. These two chapters taken together provide the ability to generate equivalent fractions and to reduce fractions to simplest terms. Chapters 4–6 deal with operations. Chapters are marked by brief concepts and explanations, followed by examples, and finally by exercises. Each chapter has a Review, to be used as a simple measure of skill attainment. A Final Assessment Test for all skills follows the last chapter.

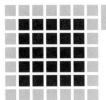

CHAPTER ONE

WHOLE NUMBERS

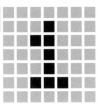

The first two chapters of *Fractions Mastery* are a quick check and refresher. Each presents simple ideas that you should easily remember. They are the 'make sure' chapters that support your preparation for the formal procedures and operations that follow.

Yes, this is a book about fractions, and fractions $\left(\frac{1}{2}, \frac{11}{15}, \frac{5}{62}, \frac{1}{100}\right)$ look very different from whole numbers (4, 57, 1,247).

For our purposes, **whole numbers** are numbers like: 0, 1, 2, 3,…10,…150,...1000,.... Whole numbers are not numbers like: $3\frac{1}{2}$, 129.6, or –7.367.

Several ideas that are applied to whole numbers can also be applied to fractions. Understanding these ideas, now with whole numbers, will help our understanding of fractions that will begin in the next chapter.

FACTORS

Factors are numbers that are multiplied together to get a **product**.

$$2 \ \times \ 6 = 12$$

factor × **facto**r = **product**

Factoring takes a number apart. There are often different factor combinations for the same product.

$$1 \ \times \ 12 \ = 12$$
$$2 \ \times \ 6 \ \ = 12$$
$$3 \ \times \ 4 \ \ = 12$$

factor × **facto**r = **product**

Listing all ways to express a number as a product yields all factors of that product.

The simplest method to find all factors for a product is to:
   1. List the whole-number combinations that produce a product.
   2. Make a list of the resulting factors.

► **Example 1**

   What factors produce 20?

       Answer: 1. List the whole-number combinations that produce 20.

           1 × 20 = 20
           2 × 10 = 20
           4 × 5 = 20

       2. Arrange the factors in ascending order.
           1, 2, 4, 5, 10, 20
      Thus, 20 has six factors: 1, 2, 4, 5, 10, 20.

► **Example 2**

What are the factors of 48?

Answer: 1. List the whole-number combinations that produce 48.

$1 \times 48 = 48$

$2 \times 24 = 48$

$3 \times 16 = 48$

$4 \times 12 = 48$

$6 \times 8 = 48$

2. Arrange the factors in ascending order.

1, 2, 3, 4, 6, 8, 12, 16, 24, 48

Thus, 48 has ten factors: 1, 2, 3, 4, 6, 8, 12, 16, 24, 48.

Factors Exercise 1: List the factors that produce the following products.

1. 4	6. 21	11. 75
2. 9	7. 24	12. 20
3. 12	8. 42	13. 124
4. 18	9. 80	14. 100
5. 19	10. 36	15. 91

Factors Exercise 2: Circle any whole numbers that are factors of the first number.

1. 6: 1 2 3 4	6. 37: 5 6 7 9	11. 45: 5 10 15 20
2. 17: 3 5 9 17	7. 32: 4 7 8 12	12. 22: 3 4 7 11
3. 27: 1 3 9 12	8. 56: 4 6 8 14	13. 105: 5 10 15 20
4. 15: 2 3 5 9	9. 49: 1 5 7 13	14. 34: 3 12 15 17
5. 8: 2 4 6 8	10. 30: 4 5 6 15	15. 51: 1 2 6 30 51

Factors Exercise 3: Answer 'yes' or 'no.'

1. Is 9 a factor of 63?	5. Is 3 a factor of 19?	9. Is 23 a factor of 23?
2. Is 6 a factor of 32?	6. Is 1 a factor of 13?	10. Is 8 a factor of 68?
3. Is 10 a factor of 130?	7. Is 7 a factor of 27?	11. Is 5 a factor of 151?
4. Is 11 a factor of 101?	8. Is 7 a factor of 59?	12. Is 12 a factor of 127?

COMPOSITE AND PRIME NUMBERS

Whole numbers can be composite numbers or prime numbers. **Composite numbers** are whole numbers that are greater than one and that have more than two factors.

36 is a composite number. It includes 1 and more than two factors.

36: 1, 2, 4, 6, 9, 10

A **prime number** is a whole number that only has two distinct factors: 1 and itself. The number 1 alone is not a prime number; it only has one factor.

17 is a prime number. Only 1 and 17 are factors:

17: 1, 17

▶ **Example**

Which are composite and which are prime numbers: 15, 19, 40, 131, 72?

Answer:	**15**	**19**	**40**	**131**	**72**
	1x15	*1x19*	*1x40*	*1x131*	*1x72*
	3x5		*2x20*		*2x36*
			4x10		*3x24*
			5x8		*4x18*
					6x12
					8x9
	1, 3, 5, 15	*1, 19*	*1, 2, 4, 5, 8,*	*1, 131*	*1, 2, 3, 4, 6, 8, 9,*
			10, 20 ,40		*12, 18, 24, 36, 72*
	Composite	*Prime*	*Composite*	*Prime*	*Composite*

Every composite number can be expressed as the product of only prime numbers. Reducing a composite number to only prime numbers is called **prime factorization**. Here are two methods for prime factorization:

PRIME FACTORIZATION: METHOD 1

Procedure: 1. Reduce the number to factors.
2. Stop with resulting prime numbers.
3. Continue reducing composite numbers until only prime numbers remain.

▶ **Example: Method 1**

Reduce 6, 12, and 72 to prime factors.

Answer:	$6 = 2 \times 3$	*2 and 3 are prime factors.*
	$12 = 4 \times 3$	*The combination of 2x6 (instead of 4x3)*
	$= 2 \times 2 \times 3$	*yields the same factors.*
	$72 = 8 \times 9$	
	$= 4 \times 2 \times 9$	*Other combinations (such as 14x3 or 2x36)*
	$= 2 \times 2 \times 2 \times 9$	*will eventually give 2x2x2x3x3.*
	$= 2 \times 2 \times 2 \times 3 \times 3$	

PRIME FACTORIZATION: METHOD 2

This procedure is just like that in Method 1, but it gives the form of a branching tree.

    1. Reduce the number to factors.

    2. Stop with resulting prime numbers.

    3. Continue reducing composite numbers until only prime numbers remain.

▶ **Example: Method 2**

    Reduce 6, 12, and 72 to prime factors.

    Answer:

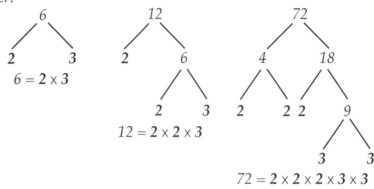

Side-by-side, here are the two methods performing prime factorization.

What are the prime factors of 54?

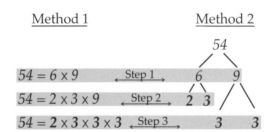

Remember, as you find the prime factors, composite numbers can have several combinations. To find the prime factors of 54, you can start with any of these choices. Each choice will eventually yield the same prime numbers:

$$54 = 2 \times 27 \qquad = 2 \times 3 \times 9 = 2 \times 3 \times 3 \times 3$$
$$54 = 3 \times 18 \qquad = 3 \times 3 \times 6 = 3 \times 3 \times 3 \times 2$$
$$54 = 6 \times 9 \qquad = 2 \times 3 \times 9 = 2 \times 3 \times 3 \times 3$$

In presenting a final list of prime factors, order the factors from smallest to largest.

$$3 \times 18 \qquad = 3 \times 3 \times 6 = 3 \times 3 \times 3 \times 2$$
$$= 2 \times 3 \times 3 \times 3$$

Factors Exercise 4: Circle all prime numbers.

1	2	3	4	5	6
7	8	9	10	11	12
13	14	15	16	17	18
19	20	21	22	23	24
25	26	27	28	29	30
31	32	33	34	35	36

Factors Exercise 5: Indicate whether the following whole numbers are prime (P) or composite (C).

1. **3**   *6.* **25**   *11.* **59**

2. **9**   *7.* **52**   *12.* **83**

3. **12**   *8.* **41**   *13.* **95**

4. **5**   *9.* **64**   *14.* **139**

5. **23**   *10.* **70**   *15.* **146**

Factors Exercise 6: Use 2 prime numbers (not including 1) that when added together equal the composite number presented. The first problem is completed as an example.

1. **5 = 2 + 3**   *5.* **24**   *9.* **58**

2. **8**   *6.* **14**   *10.* **62**

3. **12**   *7.* **30**   *11.* **44**

4. **20**   *8.* **48**   *12.* **90**

Factors Exercise 7: What is the smallest prime number, other than 1, that will divide into each of the following?

1. 8 : 2 (example)	*5.* 35	*9.* 49
2. 67	*6.* 21	*10.* 81
3. 75	*7.* 44	*11.* 53
4. 51	*8.* 121	*12.* 169

Factors Exercise 8: What is the largest prime number that will divide into each of the following?

1. 12 : 3 (example)	*5.* 51	*9.* 121
2. 14	*6.* 44	*10.* 46
3. 16	*7.* 70	*11.* 64
4. 30	*8.* 65	*12.* 300

Factors Exercise 9: Write each composite number as the product of only prime numbers.

1. 18 = 2 x 3 x 3 (example)	*5.* 46	*9.* 100
2. 48	*6.* 144	*10.* 225
3. 81	*7.* 84	*11.* 64
4. 21	*8.* 91	*12.* 248

Factors Exercise 10: Complete each factor tree.

1. 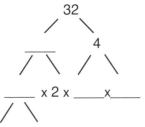 *2.* 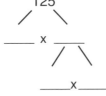 *3.*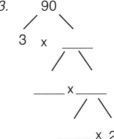

GREATEST COMMON FACTOR (GCF)

The Greatest Common Factor (GCF) helps when we compare numbers. The **GCF** is the largest factor (prime or composite) that two or more numbers share.

What is the largest (greatest) factor that 12 and 18 share?

Method 1 is the simplest method. Use these steps:

1. List the factors of each number.

2. List all factors in common.

3. Identify the largest (greatest) factor.

▶ **Example: Method 1 GCF**

Find the GCF of 12 and 18.

Answer: 1. List the factors of each number.
12: 1×12, 2×6, 3×4
1, 2, 3, 4, 6, 12
18: 1×18, 2×9, 3×6
1, 2, 3, 6, 9, 18
2. List all factors in common.
1, 2, 6
3. The largest common factor will be the GCF.
The GCF is 6. 6 is the largest factor the two numbers have in common.

Greatest Common Factor Exercise 1: Find the GCF for these pairs of whole numbers.

1. **8:**	*6.* **6:**	*11.* **7:**
12:	**4:**	**45:**
2. **3:**	*7.* **10:**	*12.* **15:**
7:	**20:**	**18:**
3. **20:**	*8.* **12:**	*13.* **6:**
25:	**32:**	**42:**
4. **6:**	*9.* **55:**	*14.* **18:**
36:	**99:**	**27:**
5. **21:**	*10.* **16:**	*15.* **28:**
42:	**24:**	**42:**

Method 1 works well with smaller numbers. It becomes more involved with larger numbers.

► **Example 2: Method 1**

Find the GCF of 64 and 80.

Answer: 1. List the factors of each number.
$$64: 1 \times 64, 2 \times 32, 4 \times 16, 8 \times 8$$
$$1, 2, 4, 8, 16, 32, 64$$
$$80: 1 \times 80, 2 \times 40, 4 \times 20, 5 \times 16, 8 \times 10$$
$$1, 2, 4, 5, 8, 10, 16, 20, 40, 80$$

2. List all factors in common.
$$1, 2, 4, 8, 16$$

3. The largest common factor will be the GCF.
The GCF is 16.

Method 2 uses composite and prime numbers to accomplish the same results.
1. Reduce all numbers to prime factors. This process is often called **prime factorization**.
2. List all prime factors that the numbers have in common.
3. Multiply the common prime numbers together to get the GCF.

► **Example 1: Method 2**

Find the GCF of 64 and 80.

Answer: 1. Reduce all numbers to prime factors.
$$64 = 2 \times 32$$
$$= 2 \times 2 \times 16$$
$$= 2 \times 2 \times 2 \times 2 \times 4$$
$$= 2 \times 2 \times 2 \times 2 \times 2 \times 2$$
$$80 = 2 \times 40$$
$$= 2 \times 2 \times 20$$
$$= 2 \times 2 \times 2 \times 10$$
$$= 2 \times 2 \times 2 \times 2 \times 5$$

Reducing the composite numbers, 64 and 80, can be done in several ways, but the results will be the same however you attack the reduction. A different reduction process might have been:
$$64 = 8 \times 8$$
$$= 2 \times 4 \times 2 \times 4$$
$$= 2 \times 2 \times 2 \times 2 \times 2 \times 2$$
$$80 = 8 \times 10$$
$$= 2 \times 4 \times 2 \times 5$$
$$= 2 \times 2 \times 2 \times 2 \times 5$$

2. List all prime factors that 64 and 80 have in common.
$$2 \times 2 \times 2 \times 2$$

3. Multiply the common prime numbers.
$$2 \times 2 \times 2 \times 2 = 16$$
$$GCF = 16$$

Method 2 will be quicker for larger numbers and when the GCF is needed for more than two numbers.

▶ **Example 2: Method 2**
   Find the GCF for 8, 16, and 24.

   Answer: 1. *Reduce all numbers to prime factors.*

   $8 = 2 \times 4$ *If you realize that 8 (2x2x2)*
   $\quad = 2 \times 2 \times 2$ *is common to all numbers, the*
   $16 = 2 \times 8$ *process is even quicker:*
   $\quad = 2 \times 2 \times 4$ $8 = 2 \times 4$
   $\quad = 2 \times 2 \times 2 \times 2$ $\quad = \mathbf{2 \times 2 \times 2}$
   $24 = 2 \times 12$ $16 = \mathbf{2 \times 2} \times 2 \times 2$
   $\quad = 2 \times 2 \times 6$ $24 = \mathbf{2 \times 2} \times 2 \times 3$
   $\quad = 2 \times 2 \times 2 \times 3$

   2. *List all prime factors in common.*
      $2 \times 2 \times 2$
   3. *Multiply the common prime numbers.*
      $GCF = 8$

Greatest Common Factor Exercise 2: Find the GCF for each set of whole numbers.

1. $4 = 2 \times 2$ 6. $56 = 2 \times 2 \times 2 \times 7$ 11. $66 = 2 \times 3 \times 11$

   $88 = 2 \times 2 \times 2 \times 11$ $6 = 2 \times 3$ $84 = 2 \times 2 \times 3 \times 7$

2. $10 = 2 \times 5$ 7. $9 = 3 \times 3$ 12. $24 = 2 \times 2 \times 2 \times 3$

   $20 = 2 \times 2 \times 5$ $27 = 3 \times 3 \times 3$ $36 = 2 \times 2 \times 3 \times 3$

   $80 = 2 \times 2 \times 2 \times 2 \times 5$ $48 = 2 \times 2 \times 2 \times 2 \times 3$

3. $9 = 3 \times 3$ 8. $15 = 3 \times 5$ 13. $50 = 2 \times 5 \times 5$

   $27 = 3 \times 3 \times 3$ $35 = 7 \times 5$ $72 = 2 \times 2 \times 2 \times 3 \times 3$

   $60 = 2 \times 2 \times 3 \times 5$ $80 = 2 \times 2 \times 2 \times 2 \times 5$

4. 24   9. 56   14. 36

   66   16   24

                                                                                        48

5. 34   10. 12   15. 100

   85   27   50

                                            42   25

Greatest Common Factor Exercise 3: Find the GCF for each set of whole numbers, using either or both methods.

1. 28	*5.* 60	*9.* 80
42	36	10
		15
2. 36	*6.* 66	*10.* 90
45	88	126
		84
3. 19	*7.* 33	*11.* 50
57	42	78
	90	112
4. 18	*8.* 27	*12.* 84
30	54	108
	108	144

COMMON MULTIPLES

You have already worked with multiples when you learned about factors.

Any whole number when multiplied by another whole number results in a multiple of that first whole number. For instance, a few multiples of 3 are:

Whole Number	Whole Number	Multiple
3	x 1	= 3
3	x 2	= 6
3	x 4	= 12

Listed in an easier form:

Multiples of 3: 3, 6, 9, 12, 15, 18, 21....

Any two numbers will share certain multiples. These shared numbers are called **common multiples**. Look for the common multiples that 2 and 3 share.

Multiples of 2: 2, 4, **6**, 8, 10, **12**, 14, 16, **18**....

Multiples of 3: 3,   **6**, 9,   **12**, 15,   **18**, 21....

Common multiples for 2 and 3 are:

6, 12, 18....

Common Multiples Exercise 1:

1. **List the first 6 multiples for:**

    a. **5:**

    b. **8:**

    c. **11:**

    d. **15:**

2. **List the first 2 common multiples of:**

a. **3:**	*b.* **6:**	*c.* **2:**
4:	**5:**	**3:**
	4:	**4:**

Understanding the Least Common Multiple (LCM) is the last whole number concept that you will need before beginning with fractions. It will become important for handling fractions.

The **Least Common Multiple** is the smallest whole number into which two or more numbers can divide evenly.

There are several methods to find the lowest common multiple. The quickest method works well with smaller numbers, like those below. Method 1 works by:

    1. Listing multiples for each number.

    2. Identifying the first number that each has in common.

▶ **Least Common Multiple: Method 1, Listing Multiples**

Find the LCM of 3 and 5. The LCM will be the first whole number greater than 0 into which 3 and 5 can divide.

    Answer: *1. List the multiples of each number.*
        3: 3, 6, 9, 12, 15, 18
        5: 5, 10, 15, 20, 25,

        2. Identify the first number that each has in common.
        3: 3, 6, 9, 12, **15***, 18*
        5: 5, 10, **15***, 20, 25,*
        LCM = 15

This 'listing multiples' method does not work well with larger numbers. For instance,

Find the LCM of 18, 27, and 30.

Listing the multiples for larger numbers is time consuming.

List the multiples of each number:

18: 18, 36, 54, 72, 90, 108, 126, 144, 162, 180, 198, 216, 234, 252, **270**
27: 27, 54, 81, 108, 135, 162, 189, 216, 243, **270**, 297
30: 30, 60, 90, 120, 150, 180, 210, 240, **270**, 300

Identify the first common number.

LCM = 270

For this reason a second method can be quicker. Besides, you have already learned the idea. Method 2 uses prime factors.

1. Reduce each number to prime factors.
2. List each prime factor AND the greatest number of times it appears in any number.
3. Multiply these prime factors together.

▶ **Least Common Multiple: Method 2, Prime Factors**

Find the LCM for 18, 27, and 30.

Answer: *1. Reduce each number to prime factors.*
$$18 = 2 \times 9$$
$$= 2 \times 3 \times 3$$

$$27 = 3 \times 9$$
$$= 3 \times 3 \times 3$$

$$30 = 3 \times 10$$
$$= 3 \times 2 \times 5$$

2. List all prime factors and their greatest occurrence.
$$2, 3, 3, 3, 5$$
Note: 2 occurs only once in 18 and 30; 3 occurs three times in 27, although it also occurs twice in 18 and once in 30; and 5 occurs once in 30.

3. Multiply.
$$2 \times 3 \times 3 \times 3 \times 5 = 270$$
$$LCM = 270$$
270 is the first number that 18, 27, and 30 have in common.

Lowest Common Multiples Exercise 1: Find the LCM for each set of numbers.

1. 3, 4
   3 =
   4 =
   LCM =

2. 2, 6
   2 =
   6 =
   LCM =

3. 4, 5
   4 =
   5 =
   LCM =

4. 15, 75
   15 =
   75 =
   LCM =

5. 6, 4
   6 =
   4 =
   LCM =

6. 4, 9
   4 =
   9 =
   LCM =

7. 9, 12
   9 =
   12 =
   LCM =

8. 5, 7
   5 =
   7 =
   LCM =

9. 7, 6
   7 =
   6 =
   LCM =

10. 6, 8
    6 =
    8 =
    LCM =

11. 21, 36
    21 =
    36 =
    LCM =

12. 8, 9
    8 =
    9 =
    LCM =

Lowest Common Multiples Exercise 2: Find the LCM for each set of numbers.

1. 9, 12, 15

2. 4, 8, 12

3. 7, 22, 84

4. 4, 5, 8

5. 8, 10, 25

6. 9, 10, 16

7. 14, 42, 49

8. 6, 75, 300

9. 30, 15, 75

10. 15, 36, 75

11. 20, 36, 48

12. 12, 16, 24

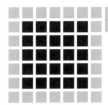
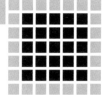

WHOLE NUMBERS

Factors. List the factors that provide the following products.

1. **6**	*4.* **20**	*7.* **91**
2. **12**	*5.* **21**	*8.* **86**
3. **17**	*6.* **75**	*9.* **124**

Composite & Prime Numbers. Are the following numbers composite (C) or prime (P)?

10. **34**	*12.* **29**	*14.* **84**
11. **54**	*13.* **139**	*15.* **59**

Write each composite number as the product of only prime numbers.

16. **48**	*18.* **21**	*20.* **144**
17. **64**	*19.* **100**	*21.* **248**

Greatest Common Factors. Find the GCF for each set of whole numbers.

22. **3**	*25.* **18**	*28.* **30**
8	**42**	**50**
23. **18**	*26.* **28**	*29.* **66**
21	**42**	**88**
24. **9**	*27.* **36**	*30.* **25**
27	**48**	**50**
81	**56**	**100**

Common Multiples. Find the LCM for each set of whole numbers.

31. **4**	*33.* **8**	*35.* **9**
5	**9**	**12**
32. **12**	*34.* **15**	*36.* **20**
16	**30**	**36**
24	**75**	**48**

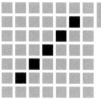
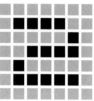
INTRODUCING FRACTIONS

A **fraction** is a ratio of two whole numbers; the top number, the **numerator**, has a relationship to the bottom number, the **denominator**.

In $\frac{5}{12}$, 5 is the numerator and 12 is the denominator.

The fraction $\frac{5}{12}$, represents the ratio of 5 parts to 12 parts. This ratio can be represented with pictures as well:

Representing fractions in picture form is helpful, but pictures are not practical for the discussions, examples, and exercises that will follow. All that follows about fractions will be presented in number forms.

Fractions with a numerator smaller than the denominator are **proper fractions**. Fractions with a numerator equal to or larger than the denominator are **improper fractions**.

▶ **Examples: Proper & Improper Fractions**

Proper Fractions	*Improper Fractions*
$\frac{1}{5}$	$\frac{7}{4}$
$\frac{8}{15}$	$\frac{37}{37}$
$\frac{29}{120}$	$\frac{120}{29}$

A **mixed number** is the combination of a whole number and a fraction.

▶ **Examples: Mixed Numbers**

$$25\frac{11}{14} \qquad 250\frac{1}{3} \qquad 15\frac{123}{250}$$

Mixed numbers can be converted into improper fractions by: 1) multiplying the denominator of the fraction by the whole number and 2) adding the numerator. The denominator will remain the same.

▶ **Examples: Converting Mixed Numbers into Improper Fractions**

Fraction denominator x whole number + fraction numerator

$$3\frac{3}{7} = \frac{24}{7} \qquad\qquad 10\frac{1}{2} = \frac{21}{2} \qquad\qquad 9\frac{3}{8} = \frac{75}{8}$$

$$7 \times 3 + 3 = \frac{24}{7} \qquad\qquad 2 \times 10 + 1 = \frac{21}{2} \qquad\qquad 8 \times 9 + 3 = \frac{75}{8}$$

An improper fraction can be converted to a mixed number by dividing the numerator by the denominator. Any remainder is expressed as a fraction.

▶ **Examples: Converting Improper Fractions into Mixed Numbers**

$$\frac{24}{7} = 7\overline{)24} \begin{array}{r} 3\frac{3}{7} \\ \hline -21 \\ \hline 03 \end{array}$$

$$\frac{21}{2} = 2\overline{)21} \begin{array}{r} 10\frac{1}{2} \\ \hline -2 \\ \hline 01 \end{array}$$

$$\frac{75}{8} = 8\overline{)75} \begin{array}{r} 9\frac{3}{8} \\ \hline -72 \\ \hline 03 \end{array}$$

Fractions Exercise 1: Identify whole numbers, proper fractions, improper fractions, and mixed numbers.

1. $\frac{17}{5}$

2. $\frac{5}{17}$

3. $3\frac{1}{2}$

4. $\frac{48}{49}$

5. $12\frac{19}{27}$

6. $124\frac{1}{3}$

7. $\frac{6}{5}$

8. $\frac{2}{1}$

9. $\frac{125}{12}$

10. $\frac{5}{5}$

11. 37

12. $\frac{12}{11}$

Fractions Exercise 2: Convert these numbers to improper fractions or if possible to whole numbers.

1. $1\frac{3}{5}$

2. $2\frac{1}{12}$

3. $14\frac{1}{3}$

4. $4\frac{3}{10}$

5. $\frac{2}{2}$

6. $10\frac{7}{8}$

7. $9\frac{2}{3}$

8. $3\frac{15}{16}$

9. $12\frac{1}{6}$

10. $\frac{37}{37}$

11. $10\frac{14}{15}$

12. $15\frac{3}{25}$

13. $17\frac{3}{8}$

14. $4\frac{11}{12}$

15. 14

Fractions Exercise 3: Convert these improper fractions to mixed numbers.

1. $\frac{5}{4}$

2. $\frac{23}{7}$

3. $\frac{29}{6}$

4. $\frac{137}{10}$

5. $\frac{131}{25}$

6. $\frac{46}{15}$

7. $\frac{105}{11}$

8. $\frac{197}{2}$

9. $\frac{113}{25}$

10. $\frac{88}{9}$

11. $\frac{17}{16}$

12. $\frac{216}{115}$

EQUIVALENT FRACTIONS

Equivalent fractions are fractions that have the same value, even though the fractions may look different.

▶ **Examples: Equivalent Fractions**

$$\frac{1}{2} = \frac{3}{6} \qquad \frac{2}{3} = \frac{6}{9} \qquad \frac{5}{8} = \frac{25}{40} \qquad \frac{5}{9} = \frac{25}{45}$$

$$\frac{6}{8} = \frac{3}{4} \qquad \frac{4}{16} = \frac{2}{8} \qquad \frac{11}{33} = \frac{1}{3} \qquad \frac{25}{125} = \frac{1}{5}$$

A technique to create an equivalent fraction is to multiply the numerator and denominator of a fraction by the same non-zero number:

▶ **Examples: Creating Equivalent Fractions**

$$\frac{1 \times 2}{2 \times 2} = \frac{2}{4} \qquad \frac{1 \times 3}{2 \times 3} = \frac{3}{6} \qquad \frac{1 \times 4}{2 \times 4} = \frac{4}{8} \qquad \frac{1 \times 5}{2 \times 5} = \frac{5}{10}$$

$$\frac{2 \times 2}{3 \times 2} = \frac{4}{6} \qquad \frac{2 \times 3}{3 \times 3} = \frac{6}{9} \qquad \frac{2 \times 4}{3 \times 4} = \frac{8}{12} \qquad \frac{2 \times 5}{3 \times 5} = \frac{10}{15}$$

$$\frac{5 \times 2}{8 \times 2} = \frac{10}{16} \qquad \frac{5 \times 3}{8 \times 3} = \frac{15}{24} \qquad \frac{5 \times 4}{8 \times 4} = \frac{20}{32} \qquad \frac{5 \times 5}{8 \times 5} = \frac{25}{40}$$

$$\frac{5 \times 2}{9 \times 2} = \frac{10}{18} \qquad \frac{5 \times 3}{9 \times 3} = \frac{15}{27} \qquad \frac{5 \times 4}{9 \times 4} = \frac{20}{36} \qquad \frac{5 \times 5}{9 \times 5} = \frac{25}{45}$$

Equivalent fractions using this multiplication idea can be listed as strings of equations.

▶ **Examples: Strings of Equivalent Fractions**

$$\frac{1}{2} = \frac{2}{4} = \frac{3}{6} = \frac{4}{8} = \frac{5}{10} = \frac{6}{12} = \frac{7}{14} \cdots$$

$$\frac{2}{3} = \frac{4}{6} = \frac{6}{9} = \frac{8}{12} = \frac{10}{15} = \frac{12}{18} = \frac{14}{21} \cdots$$

$$\frac{5}{8} = \frac{10}{16} = \frac{15}{24} = \frac{20}{32} = \frac{25}{40} = \frac{30}{48} = \frac{35}{56} \cdots$$

$$\frac{5}{9} = \frac{10}{18} = \frac{15}{27} = \frac{20}{36} = \frac{25}{45} = \frac{30}{54} = \frac{35}{63} \cdots$$

Equivalent Fractions Exercise 1: Complete these strings of equations.

1. $\dfrac{1}{4} = \dfrac{2}{} = \dfrac{}{16} = \dfrac{8}{32} = \dfrac{}{64}$

2. $\dfrac{4}{5} = \dfrac{}{10} = \dfrac{}{15} = \dfrac{16}{20} = \dfrac{20}{}$

3. $\dfrac{3}{} = \dfrac{}{40} = \dfrac{9}{} = \dfrac{}{80} = \dfrac{15}{100}$

Equivalent Fractions Exercise 2: Find equivalent fractions using multiplication.

1. $\dfrac{1 \times 3}{2 \times 3} = \dfrac{}{6}$

2. $\dfrac{1 \times}{4 \times} = \dfrac{}{16}$

3. $\dfrac{1 \times}{3 \times} = \dfrac{}{12}$

4. $\dfrac{3 \times}{5 \times} = \dfrac{}{10}$

5. $\dfrac{1 \times}{6 \times} = \dfrac{}{18}$

6. $\dfrac{3 \times}{4 \times} = \dfrac{}{8}$

7. $\dfrac{2 \times}{7 \times} = \dfrac{}{28}$

8. $\dfrac{3 \times}{10 \times} = \dfrac{}{40}$

9. $\dfrac{3 \times}{8 \times} = \dfrac{}{40}$

10. $\dfrac{7 \times}{9 \times} = \dfrac{}{54}$

11. $\dfrac{2}{9} = \dfrac{}{18} = \dfrac{}{27}$

12. $\dfrac{2}{3} = \dfrac{}{12} = \dfrac{}{18}$

13. $\dfrac{2}{5} = \dfrac{}{10} = \dfrac{}{15}$

14. $\dfrac{5}{6} = \dfrac{}{24} = \dfrac{}{36}$

15. $\dfrac{25}{100} = \dfrac{}{200} = \dfrac{}{300}$

16. $\dfrac{2}{50} = \dfrac{}{100} = \dfrac{}{150}$

17. $\dfrac{5}{8} = \dfrac{}{16} = \dfrac{}{24}$

18. $\dfrac{5}{7} = \dfrac{}{28} = \dfrac{}{35}$

19. $\dfrac{11}{12} = \dfrac{}{36} = \dfrac{}{60}$

20. $\dfrac{8}{9} = \dfrac{}{27} = \dfrac{}{36}$

21. $\dfrac{1}{2} = \dfrac{}{12} = \dfrac{}{16} = \dfrac{}{20}$

22. $\dfrac{3}{4} = \dfrac{}{16} = \dfrac{}{24} = \dfrac{}{32}$

23. $\dfrac{4}{15} = \dfrac{}{30} = \dfrac{}{45} = \dfrac{}{60}$

24. $\dfrac{7}{8} = \dfrac{}{16} = \dfrac{}{24} = \dfrac{}{32}$

25. $\dfrac{15}{16} = \dfrac{}{32} = \dfrac{}{48} = \dfrac{}{64}$

26. $\dfrac{2}{3} = \dfrac{}{12} = \dfrac{12}{} = \dfrac{}{24}$

27. $\dfrac{5}{6} = \dfrac{10}{} = \dfrac{}{24} = \dfrac{25}{}$

28. $\dfrac{1}{3} = \dfrac{}{9} = \dfrac{7}{21} = \dfrac{}{27}$

29. $\dfrac{3}{10} = \dfrac{9}{} = \dfrac{15}{} = \dfrac{}{70}$

30. $\dfrac{5}{9} = \dfrac{25}{} = \dfrac{35}{} = \dfrac{45}{}$

REDUCING FRACTIONS

Another technique to create an equivalent fraction is to divide the numerator and denominator of a fraction by the same non-zero number. This technique acts to reduce a fraction.

▶ **Examples: Reducing Fractions**

$$\frac{6 \div 2}{8 \div 2} = \frac{3}{4} \qquad \frac{12 \div 6}{18 \div 6} = \frac{2}{3} \qquad \frac{11 \div 11}{33 \div 11} = \frac{1}{3} \qquad \frac{25 \div 25}{125 \div 25} = \frac{1}{5}$$

When we work with fractions, we must often reduce them to **lowest terms**. Reducing to lowest terms makes use of the Greatest Common Factor idea (See *Method 1* and *Method 2*, pages 11–12). Here are steps to use in reducing fractions using prime factorization (*Method 2*).

1. Reduce numerator and denominator to prime numbers.
2. List the prime numbers that are common to the numerator and denominator.
3. Multiply the common prime number.
4. Use the resulting number to divide the numerator and denominator.

▶ **Example: Reducing to Lowest Terms Using Prime Factorization**

Reduce $\frac{12}{18}$ to lowest possible terms.

    Answer: 1. *Reduce numerator and denominator to prime numbers.*

$$12 = 2 \times 2 \times 3$$
$$18 = 2 \times 3 \times 3$$

2. *List the prime numbers that are common.*

$$2 \times 3$$

3. *Multiply the common prime numbers.*

$$6$$

4. *Divide the numerator and denominator by 6.*

$$\frac{12 \div 6}{18 \div 6} = \frac{2}{3}$$

$\frac{12}{18}$ *reduced to lowest terms is $\frac{2}{3}$.*

As you become more nimble with numbers, you will recognize the GCF without having to do each step suggested above.

Also remember that you can reduce to lowest terms in stages. As long as you divide a numerator and denominator by the same non-zero number at each stage, the result will be an equivalent fraction each time. This process is a slower version of prime factorization suggested above.

▶ **Example: Reducing Fractions in Stages**

Reduce $\frac{12}{18}$ to lowest terms in stages.

    Answer: $\frac{12 \div 2}{18 \div 2} = \frac{6 \div 3}{9 \div 3} = \frac{2}{3}$

This example is a two-stage reduction, dividing both numerator and denominator by 2 and then by 3.

Reducing Fractions Exercise 1: Reduce to lowest terms.

1. $\dfrac{10 \div 5}{15 \div 5} =$

2. $\dfrac{4 \div}{6 \div 2} =$

3. $\dfrac{36 \div}{40 \div} =$

4. $\dfrac{8 \div}{12 \div} =$

5. $\dfrac{27 \div}{30 \div} =$

6. $\dfrac{9 \div}{24 \div} =$

•

7. $\dfrac{15}{33} =$

8. $\dfrac{5}{50} =$

9. $\dfrac{24}{36} =$

10. $\dfrac{20}{28} =$

11. $\dfrac{25}{40} =$

12. $\dfrac{5}{15} =$

13. $\dfrac{32}{36} =$

14. $\dfrac{10}{14} =$

15. $\dfrac{36}{48} =$

16. $\dfrac{26}{52} =$

17. $\dfrac{15}{60} =$

18. $\dfrac{60}{144} =$

Reducing Fractions Exercise 2: Find the missing number in each equivalent fraction.

1. $\dfrac{3}{6} = \dfrac{1}{}$

2. $\dfrac{20}{24} = \dfrac{5}{}$

3. $\dfrac{27}{33} = \dfrac{}{11}$

4. $\dfrac{}{40} = \dfrac{3}{10}$

5. $\dfrac{28}{35} = \dfrac{4}{}$

6. $\dfrac{15}{} = \dfrac{5}{11}$

7. $\dfrac{36}{40} = \dfrac{9}{}$

8. $\dfrac{}{50} = \dfrac{9}{10}$

9. $\dfrac{25}{35} = \dfrac{}{7}$

10. $\dfrac{72}{} = \dfrac{8}{9}$

11. $\dfrac{16}{20} = \dfrac{}{10} = \dfrac{}{5}$

12. $\dfrac{4}{12} = \dfrac{2}{} = \dfrac{}{3}$

13. $\dfrac{12}{16} = \dfrac{}{8} = \dfrac{3}{}$

14. $\dfrac{56}{64} = \dfrac{}{16} = \dfrac{7}{}$

15. $\dfrac{72}{100} = \dfrac{36}{} = \dfrac{18}{}$

COMMON DENOMINATORS

Before we formally begin addition and subtraction of fractions, we need a way to compare fractions that have different denominators. Knowing about equivalent fractions will be very helpful. Suppose we must perform addition or subtraction with the fractions of $\frac{3}{4}$ and $\frac{2}{3}$. Until both fractions have a common denominator, addition or subtraction cannot be performed.

▶ **Example: Multiples, Common Denominators, and Equivalent Fractions**

Find a common denominator for $\frac{3}{4}$ and $\frac{2}{3}$, and convert each fraction into an equivalent.

Answer: 1. *List multiples for each denominator.*
2. *Determine a common denominator.*
3. *Convert both fractions to equivalents having the same denominator.*

1. *List multiples.*
$$4: 4, 8, \mathbf{12}, 16, 20....$$
$$3: 3, 6, 9, \mathbf{12}, 15....$$
2. *Determine a common denominator.*
$$12$$
3. *Convert each fraction into equivalent 12ths.*

$$\frac{3 \times ?}{4 \times ?} = \frac{?}{12}$$

$$\frac{3 \times \mathbf{3}}{4 \times \mathbf{3}} = \frac{9}{12}$$

$$\frac{3}{4} = \frac{9}{12} \text{ equivalent fractions}$$

$$\frac{2 \times ?}{3 \times ?} = \frac{?}{12}$$

$$\frac{2 \times \mathbf{4}}{3 \times \mathbf{4}} = \frac{8}{12}$$

$$\frac{2}{3} = \frac{8}{12} \text{ equivalent fractions}$$

Because $\frac{3}{4}$ and $\frac{2}{3}$ have been converted to equivalent fractions with common denominators, addition or subtraction can now take place.

This process for fractions is called finding the **least common denominator (LCD),** and it is the same idea as the **least common multiple (LCM)** that you learned earlier for whole numbers (see page 16). When used here with fractions, the LCD is the LCM for the denominators.

Adding or subtracting fractions with large denominators can be messy. So, returning to prime factorization to find the least common multiple (LCM) is helpful.

▶ Example: Prime Numbers, Common Denominators, and Equivalent Fractions

Find a common denominator for $\frac{3}{4}$, $\frac{1}{8}$ and $\frac{5}{12}$, and convert each into an equivalent fraction.

Method: 1. *Reduce each denominator to prime factors.*
          2. *List each prime factor AND the greatest number of times it appears in any number.*
          3. *Multiply these factors together to establish the LCM.*
          4. *Convert all fractions to equivalents having the same denominator.*

Answer: 1. *Reduce each denominator to prime factors.*
              4: 2×2
              8: $2 \times 2 \times 2$
              12: $2 \times 2 \times 3$
          2. *List each prime factor AND the greatest number of times it appears in any number.*
              $2 \times 2 \times 2 \times 3$
          3. *Multiply these factors together to establish the LCM.*
              $2 \times 2 \times 2 \times 3 = 24$
          4. *Convert all fractions to equivalents having the same denominator.*

$$\frac{3 \times ?}{4 \times ?} = \frac{?}{24}$$

$$\frac{3 \times 6}{4 \times 6} = \frac{18}{24}$$

$$\frac{3}{4} = \frac{18}{24} \text{ equivalent fractions}$$

$$\frac{1 \times ?}{8 \times ?} = \frac{?}{24}$$

$$\frac{1 \times 3}{8 \times 3} = \frac{3}{24}$$

$$\frac{1}{8} = \frac{3}{24} \text{ equivalent fractions}$$

$$\frac{5 \times ?}{12 \times ?} = \frac{?}{24}$$

$$\frac{5 \times 2}{12 \times 2} = \frac{10}{24}$$

$$\frac{5}{12} = \frac{10}{24} \text{ equivalent fraction}$$

Common Denominators Exercise 1: Find the lowest common denominator for each set of fractions.

1. $\frac{1}{3}$

   $\frac{1}{4}$

2. $\frac{1}{4}$

   $\frac{5}{12}$

3. $\frac{1}{5}$

   $\frac{1}{2}$

4. $\frac{1}{6}$

   $\frac{3}{10}$

5. $\frac{1}{12}$

   $\frac{4}{5}$

6. $\frac{3}{8}$

   $\frac{3}{4}$

7. $\frac{4}{5}$

$\frac{5}{12}$

$\frac{3}{20}$

8. $\frac{5}{8}$

$\frac{7}{16}$

$\frac{5}{32}$

9. $\frac{2}{9}$

$\frac{5}{27}$

$\frac{17}{54}$

Common Denominators Exercise 2: Convert each pair of fractions into equivalents that have the lowest common denominators.

1. $\frac{5}{6}$

$\frac{1}{4}$

7. $\frac{2}{9}$

$\frac{5}{12}$

13. $\frac{5}{18}$

$\frac{1}{12}$

$\frac{3}{14}$

2. $\frac{3}{8}$

$\frac{3}{4}$

8. $\frac{5}{6}$

$\frac{7}{15}$

14. $\frac{3}{10}$

$\frac{7}{30}$

$\frac{3}{20}$

3. $\frac{1}{6}$

$\frac{1}{12}$

9. $\frac{3}{7}$

$\frac{1}{5}$

15. $\frac{7}{12}$

$\frac{5}{16}$

$\frac{3}{32}$

4. $\frac{3}{8}$

$\frac{3}{16}$

10. $\frac{6}{25}$

$\frac{13}{15}$

16. $\frac{4}{15}$

$\frac{7}{45}$

$\frac{1}{30}$

5. $\frac{11}{12}$

$\frac{5}{24}$

11. $\frac{1}{3}$

$\frac{4}{9}$

$\frac{5}{6}$

17. $\frac{7}{36}$

$\frac{2}{27}$

$\frac{11}{45}$

6. $\frac{11}{15}$

$\frac{8}{9}$

12. $\frac{1}{6}$

$\frac{7}{10}$

$\frac{1}{2}$

18. $\frac{3}{8}$

$\frac{1}{4}$

$\frac{9}{10}$

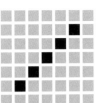
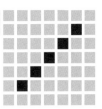

INTRODUCING FRACTIONS

Equivalent Fractions. Complete the equivalents for each string.

1. $\dfrac{1}{6} = \dfrac{}{18}$

2. $\dfrac{1}{4} = \dfrac{}{16}$

3. $\dfrac{3}{8} = \dfrac{}{40}$

4. $\dfrac{7}{9} = \dfrac{}{54}$

5. $\dfrac{5}{6} = \dfrac{}{24} = \dfrac{}{36}$

6. $\dfrac{5}{7} = \dfrac{}{28} = \dfrac{}{35}$

7. $\dfrac{11}{12} = \dfrac{}{36} = \dfrac{}{60}$

8. $\dfrac{4}{15} = \dfrac{}{45} = \dfrac{}{90}$

9. $\dfrac{2}{3} = \dfrac{}{12} = \dfrac{12}{} = \dfrac{}{24}$

10. $\dfrac{3}{10} = \dfrac{9}{} = \dfrac{15}{} = \dfrac{}{70}$

11. $\dfrac{5}{9} = \dfrac{25}{} = \dfrac{35}{} = \dfrac{45}{}$

12. $\dfrac{3}{20} = \dfrac{}{40} = \dfrac{9}{} = \dfrac{}{100}$

Reducing Fractions. Reduce to lowest Terms.

13. $\dfrac{4}{6} =$

14. $\dfrac{15}{33} =$

15. $\dfrac{9}{24} =$

16. $\dfrac{24}{36} =$

17. $\dfrac{25}{40} =$

18. $\dfrac{36}{48} =$

19. $\dfrac{26}{52} =$

20. $\dfrac{12}{100} =$

21. $\dfrac{60}{144} =$

Common Denominators. Convert each pair of fractions to equivalents having common denominators.

22. $\dfrac{1}{6}$
    $\dfrac{1}{12}$

23. $\dfrac{3}{8}$
    $\dfrac{3}{4}$

24. $\dfrac{1}{2}$
    $\dfrac{3}{8}$
    $\dfrac{5}{12}$

25. $\dfrac{4}{7}$
    $\dfrac{2}{5}$

26. $\dfrac{1}{3}$
    $\dfrac{5}{12}$

27. $\dfrac{1}{6}$
    $\dfrac{7}{10}$
    $\dfrac{1}{2}$

28. $\dfrac{2}{3}$
    $\dfrac{1}{4}$

29. $\dfrac{11}{12}$
    $\dfrac{5}{24}$

30. $\dfrac{4}{15}$
    $\dfrac{7}{45}$
    $\dfrac{1}{30}$

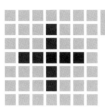
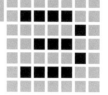
ADDITION

ADDITION WITH COMMON DENOMINATORS

Use these three steps to add fractions with common denominators:
1. Add numerators.
2. Place the sum over the common denominator.
3. Simplify, if necessary:
    a. Reduce improper fractions.
    b. Reduce all fractions to lowest terms.

▶ **Examples: Common Denominators**

- $\frac{2}{5} + \frac{2}{5}$

    1. Add numerators.

    $\frac{2}{5} + \frac{2}{5} = \frac{\mathbf{4}}{}$

    2. Place the sum over the common denominator.

    $\frac{2}{5} + \frac{2}{5} = \frac{\mathbf{4}}{\mathbf{5}}$

- $\frac{5}{11} + \frac{7}{11}$

    1. Add numerators.

    $\frac{5}{11} + \frac{7}{11} = \frac{\mathbf{12}}{}$

    2. Place the sum over the common denominator.

    $\frac{5}{11} + \frac{7}{11} = \frac{\mathbf{12}}{\mathbf{11}}$

    3. Simplify, reduce improper fraction to a mixed number.

    $\frac{12}{11} = 1\frac{1}{11}$

- $$4\frac{2}{10}$$
  $$+ \quad 1\frac{9}{10}$$
  $$\overline{}$$

    1. Add numerators, and

    2. Place the sum over the common denominator.

    $$4\frac{2}{10}$$
    $$+ \quad 1\frac{9}{10}$$
    $$\overline{5\frac{11}{10}}$$

3. Simplify, reduce improper fraction and create a mixed number.

$$4\tfrac{2}{10}$$
$$+\quad 1\tfrac{9}{10}$$
$$\overline{\qquad\qquad}$$
$$5\tfrac{11}{10} = 5 + 1\tfrac{1}{10} = 6\tfrac{1}{10}$$

-
$$\tfrac{3}{12}$$
$$+\quad \tfrac{6}{12}$$
$$\overline{\qquad\qquad}$$

1. Add numerators, and

2. Place the sum over the common denominator.

$$\tfrac{3}{12}$$
$$+\quad \tfrac{6}{12}$$
$$\overline{\qquad\qquad}$$
$$\tfrac{9}{12}$$

3. Simplify, reduce to lowest terms.

$$\tfrac{3}{12}$$
$$+\quad \tfrac{6}{12}$$
$$\overline{\qquad\qquad}$$
$$\tfrac{9 \div 3}{12 \div 3} = \tfrac{3}{4}$$

-
$$\tfrac{7}{18}$$
$$+\quad \tfrac{13}{18}$$
$$\overline{\qquad\qquad}$$

1. Add numerators, and

2. Place the sum over the common denominator.

$$\tfrac{7}{18}$$
$$+\quad \tfrac{13}{18}$$
$$\overline{\qquad\qquad}$$
$$\tfrac{20}{18}$$

3. Simplify, reduce improper fractions and reduce to lowest terms.

$$\tfrac{7}{18}$$
$$+\quad \tfrac{13}{18}$$
$$\overline{\qquad\qquad}$$
$$\tfrac{20}{18} = 1\tfrac{2}{18}$$
$$= 1\tfrac{2 \div 2}{18 \div 2} = 1\tfrac{1}{9}$$

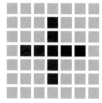
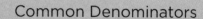
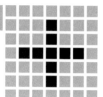

ADDITION

Reduce all answers to lowest terms, mixed numbers, and or whole numbers.

$\frac{2}{5} + \frac{2}{5} =$ $\qquad$ $\frac{1}{4} + \frac{3}{4} =$ $\qquad$ $\frac{3}{6} + \frac{3}{6} =$ $\qquad$ $\frac{5}{7} + \frac{1}{7} =$

$\frac{2}{10} + \frac{7}{10} =$ $\qquad$ $\frac{4}{9} + \frac{4}{9} =$ $\qquad$ $\frac{3}{8} + \frac{4}{8} =$ $\qquad$ $\frac{5}{11} + \frac{3}{11} =$

$\frac{10}{14} + \frac{1}{14} =$ $\qquad$ $\frac{5}{12} + 1\frac{7}{12} =$ $\qquad$ $1 + \frac{7}{8} =$ $\qquad$ $\frac{7}{10} + 2\frac{7}{10} =$

$$
\begin{array}{r} \frac{12}{15} \\ + \quad \frac{10}{15} \\ \hline \end{array}
\qquad
\begin{array}{r} \frac{5}{8} \\ + \quad \frac{3}{8} \\ \hline \end{array}
\qquad
\begin{array}{r} \frac{9}{19} \\ + \quad 8 \\ \hline \end{array}
\qquad
\begin{array}{r} \frac{5}{24} \\ + \quad \frac{6}{24} \\ \hline \end{array}
\qquad
\begin{array}{r} \frac{17}{21} \\ + \quad \frac{5}{21} \\ \hline \end{array}
$$

$$
\begin{array}{r} \frac{13}{20} \\ + \quad \frac{4}{20} \\ \hline \end{array}
\qquad
\begin{array}{r} \frac{7}{18} \\ + \quad \frac{17}{18} \\ \hline \end{array}
\qquad
\begin{array}{r} \frac{10}{11} \\ + \quad \frac{5}{11} \\ \hline \end{array}
\qquad
\begin{array}{r} 5\frac{3}{8} \\ + \quad 3\frac{4}{8} \\ \hline \end{array}
\qquad
\begin{array}{r} 10 \\ + \quad \frac{1}{2} \\ \hline \end{array}
$$

$$
\begin{array}{r} \frac{6}{8} \\ + \quad \frac{7}{8} \\ \hline \end{array}
\qquad
\begin{array}{r} \frac{12}{15} \\ + \quad \frac{11}{15} \\ \hline \end{array}
\qquad
\begin{array}{r} \frac{9}{14} \\ + \quad \frac{6}{14} \\ \hline \end{array}
\qquad
\begin{array}{r} \frac{6}{9} \\ + \quad \frac{5}{9} \\ \hline \end{array}
\qquad
\begin{array}{r} \frac{5}{7} \\ + \quad \frac{6}{7} \\ \hline \end{array}
$$

$$
\begin{array}{r} \frac{7}{12} \\ \frac{1}{12} \\ + \quad \frac{5}{12} \\ \hline \end{array}
\qquad
\begin{array}{r} \frac{7}{10} \\ \frac{9}{10} \\ + \quad \frac{3}{10} \\ \hline \end{array}
\qquad
\begin{array}{r} \frac{11}{14} \\ \frac{3}{14} \\ + \quad \frac{5}{14} \\ \hline \end{array}
\qquad
\begin{array}{r} \frac{5}{12} \\ \frac{7}{12} \\ + \quad \frac{11}{12} \\ \hline \end{array}
\qquad
\begin{array}{r} \frac{7}{9} \\ \frac{5}{9} \\ + \quad \frac{4}{9} \\ \hline \end{array}
$$

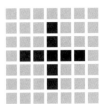
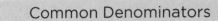
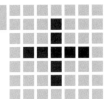

ADDITION

Reduce all answers to lowest terms, mixed numbers, and or whole numbers.

$$\begin{array}{r}\frac{1}{4}\\[4pt]+\ \frac{1}{4}\\\hline\end{array}\qquad\begin{array}{r}\frac{5}{6}\\[4pt]+\ \frac{2}{6}\\\hline\end{array}\qquad\begin{array}{r}\frac{9}{20}\\[4pt]+\ \frac{9}{20}\\\hline\end{array}\qquad\begin{array}{r}\frac{3}{8}\\[4pt]+\ \frac{3}{8}\\\hline\end{array}\qquad\begin{array}{r}\frac{5}{16}\\[4pt]+\ \frac{5}{16}\\\hline\end{array}$$

$$\begin{array}{r}\frac{3}{10}\\[4pt]+\ \frac{2}{10}\\\hline\end{array}\qquad\begin{array}{r}\frac{3}{12}\\[4pt]+\ \frac{6}{12}\\\hline\end{array}\qquad\begin{array}{r}\frac{5}{15}\\[4pt]+\ \frac{7}{15}\\\hline\end{array}\qquad\begin{array}{r}\frac{1}{12}\\[4pt]+\ \frac{5}{12}\\\hline\end{array}\qquad\begin{array}{r}\frac{1}{9}\\[4pt]+\ \frac{5}{9}\\\hline\end{array}$$

$$\begin{array}{r}\frac{7}{8}\\[4pt]+\ \frac{7}{8}\\\hline\end{array}\qquad\begin{array}{r}\frac{7}{10}\\[4pt]+\ \frac{5}{10}\\\hline\end{array}\qquad\begin{array}{r}\frac{11}{12}\\[4pt]+\ \frac{5}{12}\\\hline\end{array}\qquad\begin{array}{r}\frac{5}{9}\\[4pt]+\ \frac{7}{9}\\\hline\end{array}\qquad\begin{array}{r}\frac{9}{14}\\[4pt]+\ \frac{3}{14}\\\hline\end{array}$$

$$\begin{array}{r}\frac{13}{24}\\[4pt]+\ \frac{15}{24}\\\hline\end{array}\qquad\begin{array}{r}\frac{2}{11}\\[4pt]+\ \frac{9}{11}\\\hline\end{array}\qquad\begin{array}{r}\frac{15}{16}\\[4pt]+\ \frac{5}{16}\\\hline\end{array}\qquad\begin{array}{r}\frac{3}{4}\\[4pt]+\ \frac{3}{4}\\\hline\end{array}\qquad\begin{array}{r}\frac{14}{15}\\[4pt]+\ \frac{11}{15}\\\hline\end{array}$$

$$\begin{array}{r}\frac{5}{12}\\[4pt]+\ \frac{9}{12}\\\hline\end{array}\qquad\begin{array}{r}\frac{3}{8}\\[4pt]+\ \frac{7}{8}\\\hline\end{array}\qquad\begin{array}{r}\frac{9}{10}\\[4pt]+\ \frac{5}{10}\\\hline\end{array}\qquad\begin{array}{r}\frac{7}{12}\\[4pt]+\ \frac{7}{12}\\\hline\end{array}\qquad\begin{array}{r}\frac{11}{12}\\[4pt]+\ \frac{7}{12}\\\hline\end{array}$$

$$\begin{array}{r}\frac{3}{10}\\[4pt]\frac{7}{10}\\[4pt]+\ \frac{5}{10}\\\hline\end{array}\qquad\begin{array}{r}\frac{5}{12}\\[4pt]\frac{7}{12}\\[4pt]+\ \frac{1}{12}\\\hline\end{array}\qquad\begin{array}{r}\frac{10}{14}\\[4pt]\frac{3}{14}\\[4pt]+\ \frac{13}{14}\\\hline\end{array}\qquad\begin{array}{r}\frac{11}{18}\\[4pt]\frac{9}{18}\\[4pt]+\ \frac{10}{18}\\\hline\end{array}\qquad\begin{array}{r}\frac{10}{24}\\[4pt]\frac{15}{24}\\[4pt]+\ \frac{7}{24}\\\hline\end{array}$$

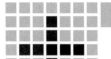

ADDITION

Reduce all answers to lowest terms, mixed numbers, and or whole numbers.

$7\frac{1}{2}$

$+ \quad 7\frac{1}{2}$

$\frac{12}{27}$

$+ \quad 5\frac{15}{27}$

$7\frac{5}{13}$

$+ \quad 6\frac{7}{13}$

$8\frac{12}{32}$

$+ \quad \frac{15}{32}$

$\frac{4}{15}$

$+ \quad 4\frac{11}{15}$

$14\frac{11}{18}$

$+ \quad 6\frac{5}{18}$

$7\frac{3}{4}$

$+ \quad 5\frac{3}{4}$

$12\frac{3}{7}$

$+ \quad 21\frac{5}{7}$

$4\frac{5}{12}$

$+ \quad 11\frac{1}{12}$

$12\frac{11}{17}$

$+ \quad 14\frac{16}{17}$

$13\frac{5}{8}$

$+ \quad 8\frac{7}{8}$

$7\frac{11}{12}$

$+ \quad 24\frac{11}{12}$

$23\frac{7}{8}$

$+ \quad 9\frac{7}{8}$

$24\frac{5}{6}$

$+ \quad \frac{5}{6}$

$9\frac{17}{32}$

$+ \quad 12\frac{25}{32}$

$7\frac{25}{64}$

$+ \quad 3\frac{31}{64}$

$28\frac{13}{15}$

$+ \quad 14\frac{12}{15}$

$30\frac{15}{20}$

$+ \quad 25\frac{17}{20}$

$8\frac{5}{33}$

$+ \quad 7\frac{6}{33}$

$3\frac{4}{5}$

$+ \quad 9\frac{2}{5}$

$15\frac{7}{18}$

$7\frac{15}{18}$

$+ \quad 12\frac{17}{18}$

$6\frac{7}{10}$

$32\frac{9}{10}$

$+ \quad 29\frac{4}{10}$

$13\frac{11}{12}$

$14\frac{9}{12}$

$+ \quad 15\frac{6}{12}$

$23\frac{17}{24}$

$25\frac{23}{24}$

$+ \quad 27\frac{16}{24}$

$7\frac{3}{15}$

$5\frac{7}{15}$

$+ \quad 3\frac{10}{15}$

ADDITION WITH UNLIKE DENOMINATORS

Use these four steps to add fractions with unlike denominators.
1. Find a common denominator.
2. Establish equivalent fractions with a common denominator.
3. Add numerators and place over the common denominator.
4. Simplify if necessary.
   a. Reduce improper fractions.
   b. Reduce all fractions to lowest terms.

▶ **Examples: Unlike Denominators**

- $\frac{3}{5} + \frac{1}{6}$

   1. *Common multiples of* $5 = 5, 10, 15, 20, 25, \mathbf{30}, 35...$

   $$6 = 6, 12, 18, 24, \mathbf{30}, 36...$$

   $$LCM = 30$$

   2. *Establish equivalent fractions with a common denominator.*

   $$\frac{3 \times 6}{5 \times 6} = \frac{18}{30}$$

   $$\frac{1 \times 5}{6 \times 5} = \frac{5}{30}$$

   3. *Add numerators and place over the common denominator.*

   $$\frac{18}{30} + \frac{5}{30} = \frac{23}{30}$$

- $\frac{3}{4} + \frac{4}{8}$

   1. *Common multiples of* $4 = 4, \mathbf{8}, 12....$

   $$8 = \mathbf{8}, 16, 24...$$

   $$LCM = 8$$

   2. *Establish equivalent fractions with a common denominator.*

   $$\frac{3 \times 2}{4 \times 2} = \frac{6}{8}$$

   $$\frac{4}{8} = \frac{4}{8}$$

   3. *Add numerators and place over the common denominator.*

   $$\frac{6}{8} + \frac{4}{8} = \frac{10}{8}$$

   4. *Simplify :*

   a. *Reduce to proper fraction.*

   $$\frac{10}{8} = 1\frac{2}{8}$$

   b. *Reduce to lowest terms.*

   $$1\frac{2 \div 2}{8 \div 2} = 1\frac{1}{4}$$

-
$$6\frac{3}{4}$$
$$+\quad 5\frac{5}{12}$$
_____

1. Prime factors of $4 = 2 \times 2$

    $12 = 2 \times 2 \times 3$

    LCM $= 4$

2. Establish equivalent fractions.

    $6\frac{3 \times 3}{4 \times 3} = 6\frac{9}{12}$

    $5\frac{5}{12} = 5\frac{5}{12}$

3. Add numerators.

    $6\frac{9}{12}$

    $+\quad 5\frac{5}{12}$
    _____
    $11\frac{14}{12}$

4. Simplify :

    a. Reduce to proper fraction.

    $11\frac{14}{12} = 12\frac{2}{12}$

    b. Reduce to lowest terms.

    $12\frac{2}{12} = 12\frac{2 \div 2}{12 \div 2} = 12\frac{1}{6}$

    $12\frac{1}{6}$

$6\frac{3 \times 3}{4 \times 3} = 6\frac{9}{12}$

$+\ 5\frac{5}{12} \quad = 5\frac{5}{12}$
_____

$6\frac{9}{12}$

$+\ 5\frac{5}{12}$
_____

$11\frac{14}{12} = 12\frac{2}{12}$

$= 12\frac{2 \div 2}{12 \div 2}$

$= 12\frac{1}{6}$

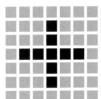
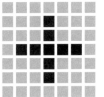

ADDITION

Reduce all answers to lowest terms, mixed numbers, and or whole numbers.

$$\begin{array}{r} \frac{1}{4} \\ + \ \frac{1}{2} \\ \hline \end{array} \qquad \begin{array}{r} \frac{1}{3} \\ + \ \frac{1}{9} \\ \hline \end{array} \qquad \begin{array}{r} \frac{5}{8} \\ + \ \frac{1}{4} \\ \hline \end{array} \qquad \begin{array}{r} \frac{1}{3} \\ + \ \frac{1}{4} \\ \hline \end{array} \qquad \begin{array}{r} \frac{1}{2} \\ + \ \frac{3}{7} \\ \hline \end{array}$$

$$\begin{array}{r} \frac{2}{5} \\ + \ \frac{3}{10} \\ \hline \end{array} \qquad \begin{array}{r} \frac{2}{15} \\ + \ \frac{3}{10} \\ \hline \end{array} \qquad \begin{array}{r} \frac{2}{5} \\ + \ \frac{1}{3} \\ \hline \end{array} \qquad \begin{array}{r} \frac{1}{8} \\ + \ \frac{1}{2} \\ \hline \end{array} \qquad \begin{array}{r} \frac{3}{4} \\ + \ \frac{1}{8} \\ \hline \end{array}$$

$$\begin{array}{r} \frac{11}{15} \\ + \ \frac{2}{5} \\ \hline \end{array} \qquad \begin{array}{r} \frac{3}{5} \\ + \ \frac{1}{2} \\ \hline \end{array} \qquad \begin{array}{r} \frac{3}{4} \\ + \ \frac{1}{3} \\ \hline \end{array} \qquad \begin{array}{r} \frac{5}{9} \\ + \ \frac{8}{8} \\ \hline \end{array} \qquad \begin{array}{r} \frac{5}{8} \\ + \ \frac{2}{5} \\ \hline \end{array}$$

$$\begin{array}{r} \frac{10}{15} \\ + \ \frac{2}{5} \\ \hline \end{array} \qquad \begin{array}{r} \frac{3}{4} \\ + \ \frac{5}{6} \\ \hline \end{array} \qquad \begin{array}{r} \frac{1}{3} \\ + \ \frac{5}{6} \\ \hline \end{array} \qquad \begin{array}{r} \frac{2}{3} \\ + \ \frac{5}{9} \\ \hline \end{array} \qquad \begin{array}{r} \frac{6}{11} \\ + \ \frac{12}{33} \\ \hline \end{array}$$

$$\begin{array}{r} \frac{15}{16} \\ + \ \frac{3}{4} \\ \hline \end{array} \qquad \begin{array}{r} \frac{3}{5} \\ + \ \frac{7}{10} \\ \hline \end{array} \qquad \begin{array}{r} \frac{3}{8} \\ + \ \frac{3}{4} \\ \hline \end{array} \qquad \begin{array}{r} \frac{1}{4} \\ + \ \frac{7}{6} \\ \hline \end{array} \qquad \begin{array}{r} \frac{5}{8} \\ + \ \frac{5}{6} \\ \hline \end{array}$$

ADDITION

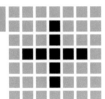

Reduce all answers to lowest terms, mixed numbers, and or whole numbers.

$$\frac{3}{10} + \frac{1}{5} \qquad \frac{2}{3} + \frac{7}{8} \qquad \frac{5}{6} + \frac{5}{9} \qquad \frac{7}{12} + \frac{2}{3} \qquad \frac{3}{4} + \frac{4}{5}$$

$$\frac{5}{6} + \frac{3}{4} \qquad \frac{7}{8} + \frac{1}{4} \qquad \frac{3}{10} + \frac{4}{15} \qquad \frac{5}{12} + \frac{5}{36} \qquad \frac{1}{4} + \frac{3}{10}$$

$$\frac{3}{8} + \frac{5}{12} \qquad \frac{2}{6} + \frac{4}{9} \qquad \frac{5}{12} + \frac{2}{3} \qquad \frac{7}{10} + \frac{4}{5} \qquad \frac{3}{5} + \frac{7}{8}$$

$$\frac{2}{3} + \frac{3}{5} \qquad \frac{7}{8} + \frac{1}{9} \qquad \frac{14}{16} + \frac{3}{4} \qquad \frac{1}{2} + \frac{9}{14} \qquad \frac{5}{6} + \frac{2}{3}$$

$$\frac{6}{12} + \frac{3}{4} + \frac{1}{3} \qquad \frac{3}{4} + \frac{3}{12} + \frac{3}{16} \qquad \frac{2}{3} + \frac{7}{15} + \frac{4}{10} \qquad \frac{1}{8} + \frac{2}{16} + \frac{2}{5} \qquad \frac{1}{2} + \frac{5}{6} + \frac{3}{4}$$

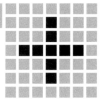

ADDITION

Reduce all answers to lowest terms, mixed numbers, and or whole numbers.

$24\frac{2}{3}$
$+ \ 17\frac{1}{2}$

$12\frac{3}{4}$
$+ \ 22\frac{3}{5}$

$42\frac{7}{8}$
$+ \ 6\frac{5}{12}$

$10\frac{5}{6}$
$+ \ 32\frac{3}{8}$

$60\frac{3}{4}$
$+ \ 16\frac{7}{10}$

$14\frac{13}{18}$
$+ \ 18\frac{4}{9}$

$24\frac{9}{10}$
$+ \ 3\frac{5}{6}$

$14\frac{3}{4}$
$+ \ 15\frac{1}{6}$

$64\frac{1}{16}$
$+ \ 38\frac{3}{8}$

$37\frac{2}{5}$
$+ \ 46\frac{1}{8}$

$3\frac{3}{8}$
$+ \ 19\frac{1}{3}$

$7\frac{1}{8}$
$+ \ 6\frac{3}{4}$

$15\frac{2}{3}$
$+ 22\frac{7}{15}$

$82\frac{9}{10}$
$+ \ 15\frac{3}{5}$

$47\frac{7}{11}$
$+ \ 12\frac{1}{3}$

$38\frac{4}{9}$
$+ \ 21\frac{3}{18}$

$37\frac{4}{5}$
$+ \ 82\frac{3}{4}$

$75\frac{7}{9}$
$+ \ 12\frac{2}{3}$

$12\frac{1}{4}$
$+ 21\frac{3}{16}$

$20\frac{17}{24}$
$+ \ 39\frac{5}{8}$

$8\frac{12}{32}$
$+ \ 9\frac{3}{8}$

$8\frac{15}{32}$
$+ 42\frac{12}{64}$

$17\frac{1}{2}$
$+ \ 14\frac{7}{8}$

$37\frac{1}{16}$
$+ \ 74\frac{3}{8}$

$39\frac{7}{10}$
$+ \ 51\frac{3}{4}$

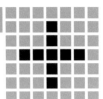

ADDITION

Reduce all answers to lowest terms, mixed numbers, and or whole numbers.

$\frac{1}{9} + \frac{3}{9} =$ $\qquad$ $\frac{3}{10} + \frac{3}{10} =$ $\qquad$ $\frac{5}{8} + \frac{3}{8} =$ $\qquad$ $\frac{7}{8} + \frac{5}{8} =$

$\frac{6}{14} + \frac{1}{14} =$ $\qquad$ $\frac{2}{9} + \frac{4}{9} =$ $\qquad$ $\frac{11}{16} + \frac{9}{16} =$ $\qquad$ $\frac{9}{19} + 8 =$

$$\begin{array}{r} \frac{12}{15} \\ + \quad \frac{10}{15} \\ \hline \end{array} \qquad \begin{array}{r} \frac{5}{8} \\ + \quad \frac{1}{4} \\ \hline \end{array} \qquad \begin{array}{r} \frac{2}{15} \\ + \quad \frac{3}{10} \\ \hline \end{array} \qquad \begin{array}{r} \frac{3}{4} \\ + \quad \frac{5}{6} \\ \hline \end{array}$$

$$\begin{array}{r} \frac{15}{16} \\ + \quad \frac{3}{4} \\ \hline \end{array} \qquad \begin{array}{r} \frac{5}{8} \\ + \quad \frac{4}{5} \\ \hline \end{array} \qquad \begin{array}{r} \frac{2}{3} \\ + \quad \frac{5}{9} \\ \hline \end{array} \qquad \begin{array}{r} \frac{5}{12} \\ + \quad \frac{2}{3} \\ \hline \end{array}$$

$$\begin{array}{r} 37\frac{1}{8} \\ + \quad 15\frac{1}{3} \\ \hline \end{array} \qquad \begin{array}{r} 3\frac{2}{3} \\ + \quad 27\frac{4}{7} \\ \hline \end{array} \qquad \begin{array}{r} 9\frac{3}{8} \\ + \quad 7\frac{12}{32} \\ \hline \end{array} \qquad \begin{array}{r} 32\frac{9}{10} \\ + \quad 18\frac{3}{5} \\ \hline \end{array}$$

$$\begin{array}{r} 17\frac{4}{9} \\ + \quad 18\frac{13}{18} \\ \hline \end{array} \qquad \begin{array}{r} 26\frac{7}{10} \\ + \quad 18\frac{3}{4} \\ \hline \end{array} \qquad \begin{array}{r} 29\frac{3}{7} \\ + \quad 29\frac{1}{2} \\ \hline \end{array} \qquad \begin{array}{r} 75\frac{2}{3} \\ + 12\frac{11}{15} \\ \hline \end{array}$$

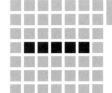
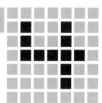

CHAPTER FOUR

SUBTRACTION

SUBTRACTION WITH COMMON DENOMINATORS

Use these steps to subtract fractions with common denominators.

1. Subtract the second numerator from the first.

2. Place the difference over the common denominator.

3. Simplify, if necessary, by reducing to lowest terms.

▶ **Example 1: Subtraction with Common Denominators**

- $\frac{15}{17} - \frac{12}{17}$

   1. Subtract the second numerator from the first.

   $$\frac{15}{17} - \frac{12}{17} = \frac{15-12}{}$$

   2. Place the difference over the common denominator.

   $$\frac{15}{17} - \frac{12}{17} = \frac{3}{17}$$

▶ **Example 2: Subtraction with Common Denominators**

- $\frac{9}{16}$

   $-\ \frac{3}{16}$

   1. Subtract the second numerator from the first, and

   2. Place the difference over the common denominator.

   $\frac{9}{16}$

   $-\ \frac{3}{16}$

   $\overline{\frac{6}{16}}$

   3. Simplify.

   $\frac{9}{16}$

   $-\ \frac{3}{16}$

   $$\overline{\frac{6 \div 2}{16 \div 2}} = \frac{3}{8}$$

Suppose there is a problem such as the following:

$$4 - \frac{3}{4} =$$

This problem has a whole number (4) from which the fraction $\left(\frac{3}{4}\right)$ must be subtracted.

A fraction must be created from the whole number in order to subtract $\frac{3}{4}$. To do this, borrow 1 from the 4. Change it into a fraction with the same denominator as $\frac{3}{4}$:

$$4 = 3\frac{4}{4}$$

▶ Example 1: Subtracting Whole Numbers and Fractions

- $4 - \frac{3}{4} = 3\frac{1}{4}$

    Explanation : Borrow 1 from 4, change it to a fraction and proceed with regular steps :

    $$4 - \frac{3}{4} =$$
    $$3\frac{4}{4} - \frac{3}{4} =$$

    1. Subtract the second numerator from the first.

    $$3\frac{4}{4} - \frac{3}{4} = 3\frac{1}{}$$

    2. Place the difference over the common denominator.

    $$3\frac{4}{4} - \frac{3}{4} = 3\frac{1}{4}$$

    Remember to include the whole number in the final answer.

▶ Example 2: Subtracting Whole Numbers and Fractions

- $$\begin{array}{r} 12 \\ -\ \frac{12}{16} \\ \hline 11\frac{1}{4} \end{array}$$

    Explanation : Borrow 1 from 12, change it to a fraction and proceed with regular steps :

    $$\begin{array}{r} 11\frac{16}{16} \\ -\ \frac{12}{16} \\ \hline \end{array}$$

    1. Subtract the second numerator from the first.

    2. Place the difference over the common denominator.

    $$\begin{array}{r} 11\frac{16}{16} \\ -\ \frac{12}{16} \\ \hline 11\frac{4}{16} \end{array}$$

    3. Simplify.

    $$\begin{array}{r} 11\frac{16}{16} \\ -\ \frac{12}{16} \\ \hline 11\frac{4 \div 4}{16 \div 4} = 11\frac{1}{4} \end{array}$$

    Remember to include the whole number in the final answer.

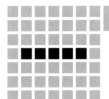
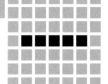

SUBTRACTION

Reduce all answers to lowest terms, mixed numbers, and or whole numbers.

$\frac{6}{7} - \frac{3}{7} =$ $\frac{3}{5} - \frac{1}{5} =$ $\frac{7}{9} - \frac{4}{9} =$ $\frac{7}{11} - \frac{4}{11} =$

$\frac{7}{8} - \frac{2}{8} =$ $\frac{17}{19} - \frac{12}{19} =$ $\frac{3}{4} - \frac{1}{4} =$ $\frac{11}{12} - \frac{3}{12} =$

$\frac{5}{9} - \frac{2}{9} =$ $\frac{17}{28} - \frac{11}{28} =$ $\frac{11}{28} - \frac{3}{28} =$ $\frac{11}{18} - \frac{7}{18} =$

$\frac{11}{15} - \frac{6}{15} =$ $\frac{13}{16} - \frac{5}{16} =$ $\frac{9}{10} - \frac{3}{10} =$ $4 - \frac{1}{2} =$

$3 - \frac{7}{16} =$ $\frac{17}{21} - \frac{8}{21} =$ $\frac{23}{25} - \frac{8}{25} =$ $15 - \frac{6}{21} =$

$$\begin{array}{r} \frac{15}{16} \\ -\ \frac{7}{16} \\ \hline \end{array} \qquad \begin{array}{r} \frac{19}{20} \\ -\ \frac{4}{20} \\ \hline \end{array} \qquad \begin{array}{r} \frac{9}{10} \\ -\ \frac{7}{10} \\ \hline \end{array} \qquad \begin{array}{r} \frac{11}{12} \\ -\ \frac{1}{12} \\ \hline \end{array} \qquad \begin{array}{r} 7 \\ -\ \frac{7}{21} \\ \hline \end{array}$$

$$\begin{array}{r} \frac{27}{30} \\ -\ \frac{15}{30} \\ \hline \end{array} \qquad \begin{array}{r} 4 \\ -\ \frac{13}{27} \\ \hline \end{array} \qquad \begin{array}{r} \frac{21}{25} \\ -\ \frac{15}{25} \\ \hline \end{array} \qquad \begin{array}{r} \frac{15}{18} \\ -\ \frac{5}{18} \\ \hline \end{array} \qquad \begin{array}{r} 8 \\ -\ 2\frac{3}{8} \\ \hline \end{array}$$

$$\begin{array}{r} \frac{10}{28} \\ -\ \frac{3}{28} \\ \hline \end{array} \qquad \begin{array}{r} 15 \\ -\ \frac{5}{12} \\ \hline \end{array} \qquad \begin{array}{r} \frac{15}{24} \\ -\ \frac{9}{24} \\ \hline \end{array} \qquad \begin{array}{r} 21\frac{3}{4} \\ -\ 16 \\ \hline \end{array} \qquad \begin{array}{r} 20 \\ -\ 17\frac{25}{30} \\ \hline \end{array}$$

SUBTRACTION WITH UNLIKE DENOMINATORS

Use these steps to subtract fractions with unlike denominators.
1. Find a common denominator.
2. Establish equivalent fractions with a common denominator.
3. Subtract numerators and place over the common denominator. If needed, borrow and create an improper fraction.
4. Simplify, if necessary, by reducing to lowest terms.

▶ Example 1: Subtracting with Unlike Denominators

- $\frac{3}{4} - \frac{1}{8}$

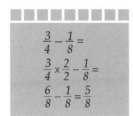

$$\frac{3}{4} - \frac{1}{8} =$$
$$\frac{3}{4} \times \frac{2}{2} - \frac{1}{8} =$$
$$\frac{6}{8} - \frac{1}{8} = \frac{5}{8}$$

  1. *Find a common denominator.*
  $$\frac{3}{4} = 4, 8, 12, 16...$$
  $$\frac{1}{8} = 8, 16, 24...$$
  $$LCM = 8$$

  In this case, one denominator (8) satisfies the other (4) as common denominator to both.

  2. *Establish equivalent fractions with a common denominator.*
  $$\frac{3 \times 2}{4 \times 2} = \frac{6}{8}$$
  $$\frac{1}{8} = \frac{1}{8}$$

  3. *Subtract numerators and place over the common denominator.*
  $$\frac{6}{8} - \frac{1}{8} = \frac{5}{8}$$

▶ Example 2: Subtracting with Unlike Denominators

- $\begin{array}{r} 15\frac{5}{6} \\ - \quad 6\frac{1}{3} \\ \hline \end{array}$

$$\begin{array}{r} 15\frac{5}{6} \\ - \quad 6\frac{1 \times 2}{3 \times 2} = \frac{2}{6} \\ \hline 9 \ \frac{3}{6} = 9\frac{1}{2} \end{array}$$

  1. *Find a common denominator.*
  $$\frac{5}{6} = 2 \times 3$$
  $$\frac{1}{3} = 1 \times 3$$
  $$LCM = 6$$
  Remember, the LCM includes each prime number AND the greatest number of times it appears.

  2. *Establish equivalent fractions with a common denominator.*
  $$\frac{5}{6} = \frac{5}{6}$$
  $$\frac{1 \times 2}{3 \times 2} = \frac{2}{6}$$

  3. *Subtract numerators and place over the common denominator.*
  $$\begin{array}{r} 15\frac{5}{6} \\ - \quad 6\frac{2}{6} \\ \hline 9\frac{3}{6} \end{array}$$

4. Simplify, if necessary, by reducing to lowest terms.

$$15\tfrac{5}{6}$$
$$-\ \ 6\tfrac{2}{6}$$
$$9\tfrac{3}{6} = 9\,\tfrac{3\div 3}{6\div 3} = 9\tfrac{1}{2}$$

The four steps work well except when the top fraction is less than the bottom fraction. This problem will occur when subtraction involves mixed numbers.

You have already been introduced to borrowing from a whole number and creating an improper fraction in order to subtract.

$$12 \quad = \quad 11\tfrac{16}{16}$$
$$-\ \ \tfrac{11}{16} \quad = \quad -\ \tfrac{11}{16}$$
$$11\tfrac{5}{16}$$

This idea of borrowing works when a larger fraction within a mixed number must be subtracted from a smaller fraction within a mixed number. Do Step 1 and Step 2. In Step 3, borrow, convert, and then subtract.

▶ **Example: Mixed Numbers and Borrowing**

•
$$15\tfrac{1}{3}$$
$$-\ \ 6\tfrac{5}{6}$$

1. Find a common denominator.
2. Establish equivalent fractions.

$$15\tfrac{1}{3} = 15\tfrac{2}{6}$$
$$-\ \ 6\tfrac{5}{6} = \ \ 6\tfrac{5}{6}$$

3. Subtract the second numerator from the first.
Borrow 1 from 15, convert it into a fraction,
add to the existing fraction.

$$15\tfrac{2}{6} = 14 + \tfrac{6}{6} + \tfrac{2}{6} = 14\tfrac{8}{6}$$

Place the difference over the common denominator.

$$14\tfrac{8}{6}$$
$$-\ \ 6\tfrac{5}{6}$$
$$8\tfrac{3}{6}$$

4. Simplify.

$$8\tfrac{1}{2}$$

$$15\tfrac{1\times 2}{3\times 2} = 15\tfrac{2}{6}$$
$$-\ 6\tfrac{5}{6}$$

$$1\overset{4}{\cancel{5}}\ \tfrac{8}{6}$$
$$-\ 6\ \tfrac{5}{6}$$
$$8\tfrac{3}{6}$$
$$8\,\tfrac{3\div 3}{6\div 3} = 8\tfrac{1}{2}$$

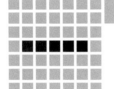

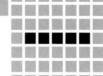

SUBTRACTION

Reduce all answers to lowest terms, mixed numbers, and or whole numbers.

$$\begin{array}{r}\frac{1}{3}\\-\frac{1}{6}\\\hline\end{array}\qquad\begin{array}{r}\frac{3}{8}\\-\frac{1}{4}\\\hline\end{array}\qquad\begin{array}{r}\frac{2}{5}\\-\frac{3}{10}\\\hline\end{array}\qquad\begin{array}{r}\frac{3}{4}\\-\frac{1}{2}\\\hline\end{array}\qquad\begin{array}{r}\frac{1}{3}\\-\frac{4}{15}\\\hline\end{array}$$

$$\begin{array}{r}\frac{2}{3}\\-\frac{1}{6}\\\hline\end{array}\qquad\begin{array}{r}\frac{1}{6}\\-\frac{1}{18}\\\hline\end{array}\qquad\begin{array}{r}\frac{1}{2}\\-\frac{3}{6}\\\hline\end{array}\qquad\begin{array}{r}\frac{9}{10}\\-\frac{1}{2}\\\hline\end{array}\qquad\begin{array}{r}\frac{3}{4}\\-\frac{1}{7}\\\hline\end{array}$$

$$\begin{array}{r}\frac{1}{2}\\-\frac{4}{9}\\\hline\end{array}\qquad\begin{array}{r}\frac{9}{10}\\-\frac{1}{6}\\\hline\end{array}\qquad\begin{array}{r}\frac{6}{7}\\-\frac{1}{3}\\\hline\end{array}\qquad\begin{array}{r}\frac{5}{7}\\-\frac{2}{5}\\\hline\end{array}\qquad\begin{array}{r}\frac{2}{3}\\-\frac{1}{15}\\\hline\end{array}$$

$$\begin{array}{r}\frac{1}{4}\\-\frac{1}{6}\\\hline\end{array}\qquad\begin{array}{r}\frac{1}{3}\\-\frac{2}{12}\\\hline\end{array}\qquad\begin{array}{r}\frac{7}{8}\\-\frac{1}{20}\\\hline\end{array}\qquad\begin{array}{r}\frac{13}{15}\\-\frac{7}{10}\\\hline\end{array}\qquad\begin{array}{r}\frac{13}{16}\\-\frac{1}{4}\\\hline\end{array}$$

$$\begin{array}{r}\frac{5}{6}\\-\frac{2}{15}\\\hline\end{array}\qquad\begin{array}{r}\frac{3}{4}\\-\frac{5}{8}\\\hline\end{array}\qquad\begin{array}{r}\frac{3}{12}\\-\frac{1}{5}\\\hline\end{array}\qquad\begin{array}{r}\frac{8}{9}\\-\frac{4}{15}\\\hline\end{array}\qquad\begin{array}{r}\frac{4}{5}\\-\frac{2}{7}\\\hline\end{array}$$

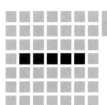
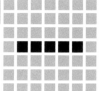

SUBTRACTION

Reduce all answers to lowest terms, mixed numbers, and or whole numbers.

$$8\frac{3}{4} \qquad 10 \qquad 7\frac{1}{5} \qquad 8\frac{5}{8} \qquad 6\frac{5}{6}$$
$$-\ 3\frac{3}{16} \qquad -\ \frac{11}{18} \qquad -\ 2\frac{2}{3} \qquad -\ 2\frac{3}{5} \qquad -\ 3\frac{1}{2}$$

$$6\frac{3}{8} \qquad 2\frac{5}{6} \qquad 2\frac{5}{9} \qquad 3\frac{3}{4} \qquad 8\frac{3}{20}$$
$$-\ 5 \qquad -\ \frac{7}{8} \qquad -\ \frac{3}{5} \qquad -\ 1\frac{2}{3} \qquad -\ 3\frac{1}{22}$$

$$7\frac{2}{9} \qquad 15 \qquad 8\frac{1}{4} \qquad 3\frac{1}{3} \qquad 19\frac{2}{8}$$
$$-\ 6\frac{2}{3} \qquad -\ 5\frac{3}{7} \qquad -\ 7\frac{8}{11} \qquad -\ 1\frac{1}{2} \qquad -\ \frac{1}{2}$$

$$9\frac{1}{14} \qquad 5\frac{1}{2} \qquad 2\frac{3}{8} \qquad 9\frac{1}{2} \qquad 8\frac{4}{6}$$
$$-\ 3\frac{3}{4} \qquad -\ 2\frac{3}{4} \qquad -\ 1\frac{4}{7} \qquad -\ 4\frac{7}{9} \qquad -\ 4\frac{3}{5}$$

$$8\frac{3}{5} \qquad 8\frac{3}{20} \qquad 6\frac{5}{6} \qquad 6\frac{1}{9} \qquad 8\frac{13}{20}$$
$$-\ 6\frac{6}{7} \qquad -\ \frac{3}{4} \qquad -\ 3\frac{7}{8} \qquad -\ 2\frac{5}{6} \qquad -\ \frac{11}{12}$$

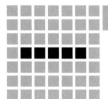

SUBTRACTION

Reduce all answers to lowest terms, mixed numbers, and or whole numbers.

$$11\frac{3}{15} - 9\frac{2}{3}$$

$$7\frac{2}{11} - 4\frac{1}{8}$$

$$23 - 17\frac{2}{5}$$

$$44\frac{11}{35} - 27\frac{9}{10}$$

$$23\frac{1}{2} - 18\frac{3}{5}$$

$$10\frac{8}{15} - 7\frac{7}{10}$$

$$14\frac{1}{2} - 13\frac{5}{6}$$

$$24\frac{17}{64} - 23$$

$$65\frac{7}{15} - 39\frac{7}{12}$$

$$15\frac{3}{16} - 14\frac{7}{8}$$

$$49\frac{5}{6} - 30\frac{6}{7}$$

$$63\frac{3}{7} - 49\frac{1}{2}$$

$$29\frac{1}{2} - 17\frac{9}{13}$$

$$45\frac{1}{3} - 29\frac{7}{8}$$

$$17\frac{3}{16} - 9\frac{21}{32}$$

$$49\frac{1}{15} - 30\frac{3}{8}$$

$$47\frac{7}{20} - 38\frac{3}{4}$$

$$21\frac{1}{12} - 17\frac{1}{3}$$

$$80\frac{3}{24} - 47\frac{13}{36}$$

$$74\frac{7}{12} - 52\frac{3}{16}$$

$$22\frac{1}{2} - 20\frac{5}{8}$$

$$72\frac{5}{6} - 27\frac{5}{8}$$

$$82\frac{9}{11} - 68\frac{21}{33}$$

$$92\frac{1}{9} - 78\frac{5}{6}$$

$$62\frac{7}{10} - 49\frac{47}{50}$$

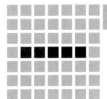
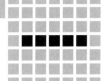

SUBTRACTION

Reduce all answers to lowest terms, mixed numbers, and or whole numbers.

$\frac{3}{7} - \frac{3}{7} =$ $\frac{7}{9} - \frac{4}{9} =$ $\frac{3}{3} - \frac{2}{3} =$ $3 - \frac{7}{8} =$

$$6 \qquad \frac{11}{12} \qquad \frac{27}{30} \qquad 21\frac{3}{4}$$
$$-\frac{13}{27} \qquad -\frac{1}{12} \qquad -\frac{15}{30} \qquad -16$$

$$\frac{1}{3} \qquad \frac{6}{7} \qquad \frac{13}{15} \qquad \frac{2}{3}$$
$$-\frac{1}{6} \qquad -\frac{1}{3} \qquad -\frac{7}{10} \qquad -\frac{5}{12}$$

$$\frac{5}{6} \qquad \frac{9}{16} \qquad \frac{3}{4} \qquad \frac{3}{12}$$
$$-\frac{2}{15} \qquad -\frac{1}{2} \qquad -\frac{5}{8} \qquad -\frac{1}{5}$$

$$13 \qquad 7\frac{1}{4} \qquad 12\frac{5}{8} \qquad 10\frac{1}{2}$$
$$-9\frac{3}{7} \qquad -6\frac{8}{11} \qquad -7\frac{3}{5} \qquad -6\frac{3}{4}$$

$$18\frac{5}{6} \qquad 47\frac{1}{9} \qquad 23\frac{5}{8} \qquad 92\frac{1}{2}$$
$$-9\frac{21}{32} \qquad -37\frac{5}{6} \qquad -17\frac{5}{6} \qquad -17\frac{3}{13}$$

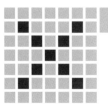

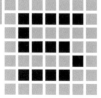

CHAPTER FIVE

MULTIPLICATION

MULTIPLYING FRACTIONS x FRACTIONS

Use these steps to multiply fractions.

    1. Multiply numerators.

    2. Multiply denominators.

    3. Reduce, if needed, to lowest terms.

▶ **Example 1: Multiplying Fractions x Fractions**

- $\frac{3}{8} \times \frac{1}{2}$

    1. Multiply numerators.

$$\frac{3}{8} \times \frac{1}{2} = 3$$

    2. Multiply denominators

$$\frac{3}{8} \times \frac{1}{2} = \frac{3}{16}$$

$$\frac{3}{8} \times \frac{1}{2} = \frac{3}{16}$$

▶ **Example 2: Multiplying Fractions x Fractions**

- $\frac{3}{4} \times \frac{2}{7}$

    1. Multiply numerators.

$$\frac{3}{4} \times \frac{2}{7} = 6$$

    2. Multiply denominators.

$$\frac{3}{4} \times \frac{2}{7} = \frac{6}{28}$$

    3. Reduce to lowest terms.

$$\frac{6 \div 2}{28 \div 2} = \frac{3}{14}$$

MULTIPLYING FRACTIONS, WHOLE NUMBERS & MIXED NUMBERS

Multiplying fractions also includes whole numbers and mixed numbers. Knowing how to change whole numbers and mixed numbers into improper fractions is helpful in multiplying.

When whole numbers and mixed numbers are to be multiplied, change whole numbers to improper fractions before going to Steps 1–3. For instance:

$$3 \times 2\frac{1}{2} = \frac{3}{1} \times \frac{5}{2}$$

▶ Examples: Multiplying Whole Numbers and Mixed Numbers

- $3 \times \frac{2}{3}$

    Change the whole number to improper fraction.

    $\frac{3}{1} \times \frac{2}{3}$

    1. Multiply numerators.

    2. Multiply denominators.

    $\frac{3}{1} \times \frac{2}{3} = \frac{6}{3}$

    3. Change improper fraction to proper fraction,
    mixed number, or whole number.

    $\frac{6 \div 3}{3 \div 3} = 2$

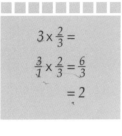

$3 \times \frac{2}{3} =$

$\frac{3}{1} \times \frac{2}{3} = \frac{6}{3}$

$= 2$

- $1\frac{2}{3} \times 5$

    Change both mixed number and whole number
    to improper fractions.

    $\frac{5}{3} \times \frac{5}{1}$

    1. Multiply numerators.

    2. Multiply denominators.

    $\frac{5}{3} \times \frac{5}{1} = \frac{25}{3}$

    3. Change improper fraction to proper fraction
    or mixed number.

    $\frac{25}{3} = 8\frac{1}{3}$

$1\frac{2}{3} \times 5 =$

$\frac{5}{3} \times \frac{5}{1} = \frac{25}{3}$

$= 8\frac{1}{8}$

- $2\frac{1}{3} \times 4\frac{1}{4}$

    Change both mixed number and whole number
    to improper fractions.

    $\frac{7}{3} \times \frac{17}{4}$

    1. Multiply numerators.

    2. Multiply denominators.

    $\frac{7}{3} \times \frac{17}{4} = \frac{119}{12}$

    3. Change improper fraction to proper fraction
    or mixed number.

    $\frac{119}{12} = 9\frac{11}{12}$

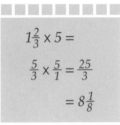

$2\frac{1}{3} \times 4\frac{1}{4} =$

$\frac{7}{3} \times \frac{17}{4} = \frac{119}{12}$

$= 9\frac{11}{12}$

CROSS CANCELLATION

Here is a short cut that is very helpful in the multiplication of fractions. The idea will also work well for division of fractions, in the next chapter. It reduces work, using your knowledge of factors and division. Yes, it may seem out-of-place to include division here in a chapter about multiplication, but cross cancellation is a helpful technique.

Cross cancellation eliminates common factors and avoids the need to multiply large numbers. It also eliminates the need to reduce answer.

Use these steps to cross cancel:

    1. Cancel factors shared by opposite numerators and by opposite denominators.

    2. Multiply the numerators.

    3. Multiply the denominators.

    4. Reduce to lowest terms.

▶ **Example: Cross Cancellation**

- $3\frac{6}{7} \times 2\frac{1}{3}$

  Change mixed numbers to improper fractions.

  $$3\frac{6}{7} \times 2\frac{1}{3} = \frac{27}{7} \times \frac{7}{3}$$

  1. Cancel factors shared by opposite numerators and denominators.

  $$3\frac{6}{7} \times 2\frac{1}{3} = \frac{\overset{9}{\cancel{27}}}{\underset{1}{\cancel{7}}} \times \frac{\overset{1}{\cancel{7}}}{\underset{1}{\cancel{3}}}$$

  3 is a cross factor of 27 and 3. $27 \div 3 = 9$ and $3 \div 3 = 1$.

  $$\frac{\overset{9}{\cancel{27}}}{7} \times \frac{7}{\underset{1}{\cancel{3}}}$$

  7 is a cross factor of 7 and 7. $7 \div 7 = 1$ and $7 \div 7 = 1$.

  $$\frac{27}{\underset{1}{\cancel{7}}} \times \frac{\overset{1}{\cancel{7}}}{3}$$

  2. Multiply the numerators.

  3. Multiply the denominators.

  $$\frac{9}{1} \times \frac{1}{1} = \frac{9}{1}$$

  4. Reduce.

  $$\frac{9}{1} = 9$$

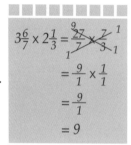

$$3\frac{6}{7} \times 2\frac{1}{3} = \frac{\overset{9}{\cancel{27}}}{\underset{1}{\cancel{7}}} \times \frac{\overset{1}{\cancel{7}}}{\underset{1}{\cancel{3}}}$$
$$= \frac{9}{1} \times \frac{1}{1}$$
$$= \frac{9}{1}$$
$$= 9$$

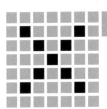
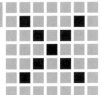

MULTIPLICATION

Reduce all answers to lowest terms, mixed numbers, and or whole numbers.

$\frac{1}{2} \times \frac{1}{4} =$ $\frac{2}{7} \times \frac{6}{7} =$ $\frac{3}{7} \times \frac{1}{4} =$ $\frac{1}{3} \times \frac{1}{5} =$

$\frac{3}{8} \times \frac{1}{2} =$ $\frac{1}{4} \times \frac{3}{16} =$ $\frac{3}{8} \times \frac{5}{8} =$ $\frac{4}{5} \times \frac{2}{3} =$

$\frac{3}{4} \times \frac{2}{7} =$ $\frac{2}{5} \times \frac{5}{8} =$ $\frac{7}{10} \times \frac{5}{6} =$ $\frac{4}{5} \times \frac{15}{16} =$

$\frac{7}{9} \times \frac{3}{7} =$ $\frac{5}{6} \times \frac{3}{5} =$ $\frac{1}{12} \times \frac{4}{5} =$ $\frac{9}{12} \times \frac{3}{4} =$

$\frac{4}{11} \times \frac{3}{16} =$ $\frac{1}{4} \times \frac{8}{9} =$ $\frac{9}{10} \times \frac{2}{3} =$ $\frac{5}{6} \times \frac{2}{7} =$

$\frac{8}{12} \times \frac{3}{4} =$ $\frac{5}{8} \times \frac{2}{3} =$ $\frac{3}{4} \times \frac{8}{9} =$ $\frac{2}{5} \times \frac{7}{9} =$

$\frac{3}{8} \times \frac{1}{9} =$ $\frac{1}{4} \times \frac{6}{11} =$ $\frac{2}{3} \times \frac{1}{9} =$ $\frac{3}{10} \times \frac{7}{10} =$

$\frac{4}{5} \times \frac{1}{8} =$ $\frac{8}{15} \times \frac{2}{3} =$ $\frac{5}{6} \times \frac{3}{8} =$ $\frac{5}{12} \times \frac{7}{10} =$

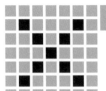

MULTIPLICATION

Reduce all answers to lowest terms, mixed numbers, and or whole numbers.

$\frac{3}{5} \times 5 =$ $\frac{5}{8} \times 12 =$ $\frac{7}{10} \times 96 =$ $6 \times \frac{7}{8} =$

$24 \times \frac{11}{12} =$ $2\frac{3}{4} \times \frac{5}{6} =$ $\frac{2}{3} \times 2\frac{11}{12} =$ $\frac{15}{16} \times 1\frac{1}{3} =$

$3\frac{1}{2} \times \frac{4}{9} =$ $10 \times 10\frac{1}{10} =$ $2\frac{5}{6} \times 1\frac{2}{3} =$ $1\frac{1}{3} \times 1\frac{1}{3} =$

$2\frac{2}{3} \times 2\frac{7}{12} =$ $1\frac{1}{2} \times 3\frac{2}{3} =$ $2\frac{1}{2} \times 6\frac{1}{3} =$ $1\frac{2}{3} \times 2\frac{4}{5} =$

$2\frac{1}{4} \times 2\frac{2}{3} =$ $2\frac{2}{7} \times 2\frac{5}{8} =$ $4\frac{1}{8} \times 5\frac{1}{3} =$ $4\frac{1}{6} \times 2\frac{5}{8} =$

$5\frac{2}{5} \times 7\frac{1}{3} =$ $3\frac{1}{8} \times 4\frac{3}{8} =$ $6\frac{3}{7} \times 6\frac{1}{2} =$ $8\frac{1}{2} \times 1\frac{1}{4} =$

$3\frac{1}{10} \times 5\frac{1}{2} =$ $4\frac{3}{5} \times 4\frac{3}{8} =$ $2\frac{3}{10} \times 1\frac{1}{7} =$ $4\frac{1}{6} \times 2\frac{2}{5} =$

$3\frac{5}{6} \times 7\frac{1}{4} =$ $8\frac{9}{10} \times 7\frac{3}{8} =$ $3\frac{11}{12} \times 7\frac{1}{8} =$ $10\frac{2}{3} \times 7\frac{3}{8} =$

MULTIPLICATION

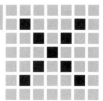

Reduce all answers to lowest terms, mixed numbers, and or whole numbers.

$8\frac{1}{5} \times 1\frac{1}{4} =$ $\qquad$ $3\frac{3}{4} \times 3\frac{1}{6} =$ $\qquad$ $6\frac{3}{7} \times 6\frac{1}{5} =$ $\qquad$ $2\frac{2}{7} \times 2\frac{7}{8} =$

$1\frac{1}{2} \times 3\frac{7}{8} =$ $\qquad$ $2\frac{2}{5} \times 6\frac{3}{8} =$ $\qquad$ $12\frac{1}{3} \times 2\frac{3}{5} =$ $\qquad$ $1\frac{1}{2} \times 3\frac{3}{3} =$

$3\frac{3}{5} \times 2\frac{5}{6} =$ $\qquad$ $8\frac{2}{5} \times 6\frac{1}{2} =$ $\qquad$ $4\frac{3}{4} \times 1\frac{1}{3} =$ $\qquad$ $5\frac{2}{3} \times 4\frac{1}{8} =$

$2\frac{3}{4} \times 3\frac{1}{3} =$ $\qquad$ $5\frac{1}{5} \times 7\frac{1}{2} =$ $\qquad$ $2\frac{5}{6} \times 7\frac{1}{3} =$ $\qquad$ $2\frac{1}{2} \times 4\frac{4}{5} =$

$7\frac{7}{9} \times 4\frac{2}{6} =$ $\qquad$ $2\frac{2}{3} \times 3\frac{1}{2} =$ $\qquad$ $3\frac{5}{9} \times 1\frac{2}{3} =$ $\qquad$ $4\frac{3}{8} \times 7\frac{3}{4} =$

$3\frac{5}{6} \times 6\frac{7}{8} =$ $\qquad$ $9\frac{3}{5} \times 1\frac{2}{3} =$ $\qquad$ $7\frac{5}{8} \times 3\frac{1}{2} =$ $\qquad$ $14\frac{1}{5} \times 7\frac{1}{2} =$

$3\frac{1}{2} \times 2\frac{8}{9} =$ $\qquad$ $7\frac{3}{4} \times 5\frac{2}{3} =$ $\qquad$ $8\frac{1}{2} \times 4\frac{1}{3} =$ $\qquad$ $2\frac{1}{8} \times 4\frac{2}{3} =$

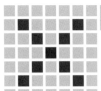
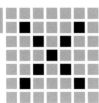

MULTIPLICATION

Reduce all answers to lowest terms, mixed numbers, and or whole numbers.

$\frac{3}{8} \times \frac{1}{2} =$ $\frac{2}{3} \times \frac{3}{4} =$ $\frac{1}{12} \times \frac{4}{5} =$ $\frac{6}{7} \times \frac{5}{6} =$

$\frac{3}{11} \times \frac{22}{27} =$ $\frac{4}{5} \times \frac{1}{8} =$ $\frac{7}{9} \times \frac{18}{35} =$ $\frac{8}{15} \times \frac{3}{10} =$

$\frac{7}{8} \times 8 =$ $\frac{7}{10} \times 96 =$ $16 \times 7\frac{5}{12} =$ $25 \times \frac{1}{25} =$

$5\frac{1}{4} \times 2\frac{5}{7} =$ $2\frac{11}{12} \times \frac{2}{3} =$ $2\frac{1}{4} \times 2\frac{2}{3} =$ $8\frac{1}{2} \times 1\frac{1}{4} =$

$6\frac{3}{4} \times 5\frac{2}{3} =$ $2\frac{1}{9} \times 3\frac{4}{5} =$ $4\frac{2}{3} \times \frac{1}{9} =$ $7\frac{1}{2} \times 3\frac{1}{3} =$

$4\frac{2}{5} \times 6\frac{1}{2} =$ $10\frac{2}{3} \times 8\frac{3}{8} =$ $2\frac{2}{7} \times 2\frac{7}{8} =$ $10\frac{1}{2} \times 6\frac{1}{3} =$

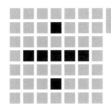 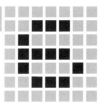

CHAPTER SIX

DIVISION

RECIPROCALS

Dividing fractions is very much like multiplying fractions. The important difference is the use of reciprocals. **Reciprocals** are two numbers that when multiplied together equal 1.

The reciprocal of $\frac{1}{2}$ is $\frac{2}{1}$. The reciprocal of 3 is $\frac{1}{3}$.

Finding a reciprocal is simply turning a number or fraction upside down:

$\frac{6}{7}: \frac{6}{7} \times \frac{7}{6} = 1$ $8: \frac{8}{1} \times \frac{1}{8} = 1$ $2\frac{1}{2}: \frac{5}{2} \times \frac{2}{5} = 1$

Use these steps to divide fractions.
1. Change the second fraction, mixed number, or whole number to its reciprocal.
2. Multiply the first fraction by the reciprocal of the second fraction.
3. Place in lowest terms.

▶ Examples: Reciprocals and Dividing

- $\frac{2}{3} \div \frac{1}{4}$

   1. Change the second fraction to its reciprocal.
      The reciprocal of $\frac{1}{4}$ is $\frac{4}{1}$.
   2. Multiply the first fraction by the second.
      $\frac{2}{3} \times \frac{4}{1} = \frac{8}{3}$
   3. Reduce to lowest terms.
      $\frac{8}{3} = 2\frac{2}{3}$

   $\frac{2}{3} \div \frac{1}{4} =$

   $\frac{2}{3} \times \frac{4}{1} = \frac{8}{3}$

   $= 2\frac{2}{3}$

- $1\frac{5}{8} \div 7$

   1. Change the second number to its reciprocal.
      The reciprocal of 7 is $\frac{1}{7}$.
   2. Multiply the first fraction by the second.
      $\frac{13}{8} \times \frac{1}{7} = \frac{13}{56}$

   $1\frac{5}{8} \div 7 =$

   $\frac{13}{8} \times \frac{1}{7} = \frac{13}{56}$

- $3\frac{5}{6} \div 2\frac{2}{3}$

   1. Change the second mixed number to its reciprocal.
      The reciprocal of $\frac{8}{3}$ is $\frac{3}{8}$.
   2. Multiply the first fraction by the second.
      $\frac{23}{6} \times \frac{3}{8} = \frac{69}{48}$
   3. Reduce to lowest terms.
      $\frac{69}{48} = 1\frac{21}{48} = 1\frac{7}{16}$

   $3\frac{5}{6} \div 2\frac{2}{3} =$

   $\frac{23}{\underset{2}{6}} \times \frac{\overset{1}{3}}{8} = \frac{23}{16}$

   $= 1\frac{7}{16}$

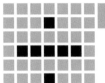
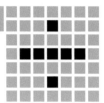

DIVISION

Reduce all answers to lowest terms, mixed numbers, and or whole numbers.

$\frac{1}{3} \div \frac{1}{2} =$ 　　　　$\frac{1}{3} \div \frac{3}{4} =$ 　　　　$\frac{2}{3} \div \frac{3}{4} =$ 　　　　$\frac{1}{4} \div \frac{1}{4} =$

$\frac{1}{2} \div \frac{4}{5} =$ 　　　　$\frac{3}{8} \div \frac{2}{5} =$ 　　　　$\frac{1}{4} \div \frac{1}{2} =$ 　　　　$\frac{3}{16} \div \frac{2}{3} =$

$\frac{1}{8} \div \frac{1}{4} =$ 　　　　$\frac{5}{8} \div \frac{5}{6} =$ 　　　　$\frac{1}{4} \div \frac{3}{4} =$ 　　　　$\frac{4}{5} \div \frac{8}{9} =$

$\frac{1}{8} \div \frac{7}{8} =$ 　　　　$\frac{3}{4} \div \frac{3}{8} =$ 　　　　$\frac{1}{3} \div \frac{2}{3} =$ 　　　　$\frac{1}{10} \div \frac{2}{5} =$

$\frac{2}{3} \div \frac{2}{5} =$ 　　　　$\frac{4}{5} \div \frac{3}{4} =$ 　　　　$\frac{5}{6} \div \frac{2}{7} =$ 　　　　$\frac{3}{5} \div \frac{1}{12} =$

$\frac{4}{7} \div \frac{3}{7} =$ 　　　　$\frac{7}{10} \div \frac{3}{4} =$ 　　　　$\frac{2}{5} \div \frac{15}{16} =$ 　　　　$\frac{3}{8} \div \frac{4}{15} =$

$\frac{13}{20} \div \frac{1}{2} =$ 　　　　$\frac{5}{6} \div \frac{7}{9} =$ 　　　　$\frac{3}{5} \div \frac{9}{10} =$ 　　　　$\frac{6}{7} \div \frac{5}{21} =$

$\frac{11}{12} \div \frac{5}{6} =$ 　　　　$\frac{4}{5} \div \frac{1}{8} =$ 　　　　$\frac{3}{4} \div \frac{5}{8} =$ 　　　　$\frac{8}{9} \div \frac{4}{5} =$

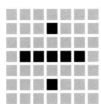 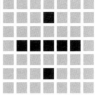
DIVISION

Reduce all answers to lowest terms, mixed numbers, and or whole numbers.

$\frac{17}{20} \div \frac{3}{4} =$ $\frac{1}{2} \div 2 =$ $\frac{9}{25} \div \frac{6}{75} =$ $2 \div \frac{2}{7} =$

$8 \div \frac{1}{10} =$ $\frac{3}{4} \div 2 =$ $\frac{24}{33} \div \frac{2}{11} =$ $\frac{12}{10} \div \frac{11}{20} =$

$1\frac{1}{2} \div 5 =$ $2\frac{1}{4} \div \frac{1}{2} =$ $\frac{3}{4} \div 4\frac{1}{8} =$ $3\frac{3}{8} \div \frac{1}{4} =$

$2\frac{1}{2} \div 1\frac{1}{4} =$ $4\frac{2}{3} \div \frac{7}{8} =$ $1\frac{5}{8} \div 1\frac{1}{4} =$ $7\frac{1}{3} \div 11 =$

$3\frac{1}{2} \div 4\frac{1}{2} =$ $5\frac{1}{2} \div 1\frac{5}{6} =$ $4\frac{1}{3} \div 26 =$ $6\frac{2}{5} \div 2\frac{1}{5} =$

$2\frac{1}{4} \div 1\frac{1}{2} =$ $2\frac{1}{7} \div 1\frac{2}{3} =$ $14 \div 14\frac{1}{2} =$ $1\frac{4}{5} \div \frac{3}{10} =$

$3\frac{1}{2} \div 2\frac{2}{8} =$ $1\frac{2}{3} \div 2\frac{5}{8} =$ $2\frac{3}{8} \div 1\frac{1}{4} =$ $3\frac{1}{9} \div 2\frac{2}{5} =$

$12\frac{1}{2} \div 6\frac{1}{4} =$ $3\frac{8}{9} \div 3\frac{1}{3} =$ $4\frac{1}{8} \div 11 =$ $1\frac{3}{7} \div 3\frac{4}{5} =$

$5\frac{1}{6} \div 6\frac{8}{9} =$ $10\frac{1}{2} \div \frac{7}{12} =$ $3\frac{1}{9} \div 2\frac{2}{5} =$ $12\frac{5}{6} \div 8\frac{2}{3} =$

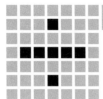
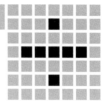

DIVISION

Reduce all answers to lowest terms, mixed numbers, and or whole numbers.

$\frac{1}{6} \div \frac{1}{6} =$ $\frac{2}{3} \div \frac{3}{4} =$ $\frac{1}{5} \div \frac{1}{4} =$ $\frac{3}{8} \div \frac{4}{15} =$

$\frac{3}{16} \div 3 =$ $10 \div \frac{1}{2} =$ $1\frac{1}{2} \div 5 =$ $8\frac{6}{7} \div \frac{3}{8} =$

$\frac{17}{20} \div \frac{3}{4} =$ $2\frac{1}{4} \div \frac{1}{2} =$ $\frac{12}{10} \div \frac{11}{20} =$ $1\frac{7}{10} \div \frac{4}{5} =$

$3\frac{3}{8} \div \frac{1}{4} =$ $\frac{1}{2} \div 3\frac{1}{3} =$ $\frac{24}{33} \div 2\frac{1}{5} =$ $2\frac{1}{8} \div 17 =$

$7\frac{1}{5} \div 2\frac{3}{5} =$ $1\frac{5}{7} \div 4\frac{2}{7} =$ $3\frac{3}{8} \div 1\frac{7}{8} =$ $5\frac{7}{8} \div 5\frac{3}{4} =$

$1\frac{2}{4} \div 4\frac{1}{4} =$ $5\frac{1}{3} \div 1\frac{5}{8} =$ $4\frac{5}{7} \div 4\frac{5}{7} =$ $4\frac{3}{7} \div 1\frac{1}{2} =$

$3\frac{1}{3} \div 9\frac{2}{5} =$ $8\frac{2}{5} \div 3\frac{8}{9} =$ $6\frac{3}{7} \div 2\frac{1}{5} =$ $4\frac{1}{2} \div 8\frac{1}{2} =$

$3\frac{8}{9} \div 3\frac{1}{3} =$ $1\frac{2}{3} \div 4\frac{1}{6} =$ $8\frac{2}{3} \div 6\frac{1}{2} =$ $6\frac{1}{3} \div 4\frac{5}{12} =$

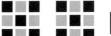 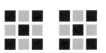

Reduce all answers to lowest terms, mixed numbers, and or whole numbers.

$\frac{11}{16} + \frac{11}{16} =$

$2\frac{3}{4} + 2\frac{3}{4} =$

$\begin{array}{r} \frac{1}{3} \\ + \quad \frac{3}{7} \\ \hline \end{array}$

$\begin{array}{r} 3\frac{2}{5} \\ + \quad 4\frac{1}{6} \\ \hline \end{array}$

$\begin{array}{r} 9\frac{1}{3} \\ + \quad 6\frac{7}{15} \\ \hline \end{array}$

$\begin{array}{r} 8\frac{3}{5} \\ + \quad 7\frac{5}{8} \\ \hline \end{array}$

$\frac{3}{4} - \frac{1}{4} =$

$\frac{11}{12} - \frac{7}{12} =$

$\begin{array}{r} \frac{3}{5} \\ - \quad \frac{1}{2} \\ \hline \end{array}$

$\begin{array}{r} \frac{5}{6} \\ - \quad \frac{5}{12} \\ \hline \end{array}$

$\begin{array}{r} 10\frac{3}{7} \\ - \quad 7\frac{2}{3} \\ \hline \end{array}$

$\begin{array}{r} 23\frac{5}{8} \\ - \quad 17\frac{3}{4} \\ \hline \end{array}$

$\frac{4}{7} \times 21 =$

$\frac{3}{4} \times \frac{2}{3} =$

$2\frac{3}{4} \times \frac{1}{2} =$

$2\frac{1}{4} \times 2\frac{1}{4} =$

$\frac{15}{16} \times \frac{4}{5} =$

$3\frac{5}{6} \times 1\frac{3}{5} =$

$1\frac{3}{10} \times 3\frac{1}{5} =$

$\frac{1}{3} \times 14\frac{1}{4} =$

$\frac{1}{3} \div \frac{1}{2} =$

$\frac{1}{4} \div \frac{1}{2} =$

$\frac{5}{9} \div \frac{1}{7} =$

$\frac{11}{12} \div \frac{5}{6} =$

$\frac{3}{4} \div 2 =$

$2\frac{1}{4} \div \frac{1}{2} =$

$3\frac{1}{2} \div 2\frac{5}{8} =$

$12\frac{5}{6} \div 8\frac{2}{3} =$